What People Are S
Threshold Bibl~ ~~~~~~~

"This remarkable series provides a method of study and reflection that is bound to produce rich fruit."   Dianne Bergant, CSA, Catholic Theological Union, Chicago

"This fine series will provide needed tools that can deepen your understanding of Scripture, but most importantly it can deepen your faith."
     Most Reverend Charles J. Chaput, OFM Cap, Archbishop of Denver

"Threshold Bible Study is a wonderful series that helps modern people read the Bible with insight and joy."   Richard J. Clifford, SJ, Weston Jesuit School of Theology

"The commentary of Stephen Binz does far more than inform; it asks for commitment and assent on the part of the reader/prayer."
     Kathleen O'Connell Chesto, author of F.I.R.E. and Why Are the Dandelions Weeds?

"This is a wonderful gift for those wishing to make a home for the Word in their hearts."
     Carol J. Dempsey, OP, Associate Professor of Theology,
     University of Portland, OR

"Written in a sprightly easy-to-understand style, these volumes will engage the mind, heart, and spirit."   Alexander A. Di Lella, OFM, The Catholic University of America

"By covering a wide variety of themes and topics, Threshold Bible Study continually breathes new life into ancient texts."
     John R. Donahue, SJ, St. Mary's Seminary and University

"Threshold Bible Study successfully bridges the painful gap between solid biblical scholarship and the rich spiritual nourishment that we expect to find in the words of Scripture."
     Demetrius Dumm, OSB, Saint Vincent Archabbey

"Threshold Bible Study offers a marvelous new approach for individuals and groups to study themes in our rich biblical and theological tradition."
     John Endres, SJ, Jesuit School of Theology, Berkeley

"Threshold Bible Study enables Catholics to read, with greater understanding, the Bible in the Church."   Francis Cardinal George, OMI, Archbishop of Chicago

"Threshold Bible Study offers you an encounter with the Word that will make your heart come alive."   Tim Gray, Director of the Denver Catholic Biblical School

"Threshold Bible Study offers solid scholarship and spiritual depth."
Scott Hahn, Franciscan University of Steubenville

"Threshold Bible Study offers those who want to begin faith-filled and prayerful study of the Bible with a user-friendly tool." Leslie J. Hoppe, OFM, Catholic Theological Union

"Threshold Bible Study is a fine blend of the best of biblical scholarship and a realistic sensitivity to the spiritual journey of the believing Christian."
Francis J. Moloney, SDB, The Catholic University of America

"An invaluable guide that can make reading the Bible enjoyable and truly nourishing."
Jacques Nieuviarts, Institut Catholique de Toulouse

"Threshold Bible Study is a refreshing approach to enable participants to ponder the Scriptures more deeply." Irene Nowell, OSB, Mount St. Scholastica

"Threshold Bible Study stands in the tradition of the biblical renewal movement and brings it back to life." Kathleen M. O'Connor, Columbia Theological Seminary

"This series is exceptional for its scholarly solidity, pastoral practicality, and clarity of presentation." Peter C. Phan, Georgetown University

"Threshold Bible Study is the perfect series of Bible study books for serious students with limited time." John J. Pilch, Georgetown University

"These thematic books are informative, easy to use, rooted in the Church's tradition of reflection and prayer, and of sound catechetical method."
Most Reverend Anthony M. Pilla, Bishop of Cleveland

"Threshold Bible Study is an enriching and enlightening approach to understanding the rich faith which the Scriptures hold for us today." Abbot Gregory J. Polan, OSB,
Conception Abbey and Seminary College

"Threshold Bible Study leads the reader from Bible study to personal prayer, community involvement, and active Christian commitment in the world."
Sandra M. Schneiders, Jesuit School of Theology, Berkeley

"This is the best material I have seen for serious Bible study."
Most Reverend Donald W. Trautman, Bishop of Erie

"Guaranteed to make your love of Scripture grow!"
Ronald D. Witherup, SS, author of The Bible Companion

The RESURRECTION *& The* LIFE

Stephen J. Binz

Third printing 2012

TWENTY-THIRD PUBLICATIONS
A Division of Bayard
One Montauk Avenue, Suite 200
New London, CT 06320
(860) 437-3012 or (800) 321-0411
www.23rdpublications.com

Copyright ©2006 Stephen J. Binz. All rights reserved. No part of this publication may be reproduced in any manner without prior written permission of the publisher. Write to the Permissions Editor.

The Scripture passages contained herein are from the *New Revised Standard Version of the Bible*, Catholic edition. Copyright ©1989, by the Division of Christian Education of the National Council of Churches in the U.S.A. All rights reserved.

ISBN 978-1-58595-367-7
Library of Congress: 2005929693
Printed in the U.S.A.

Contents

How to Use
Threshold Bible Study

Each book in the Threshold Bible Study series is designed to lead you through a new doorway of biblical awareness, to accompany you across a unique threshold of understanding. The characters, places, and images that you encounter in each of these topical studies will help you explore fresh dimensions of your faith and discover richer insights for your spiritual life.

Threshold Bible Study covers biblical themes in depth in a short amount of time. Unlike more traditional Bible studies that treat a biblical book or series of books, Threshold Bible Study aims to address specific topics within the entire Bible. The goal is not for you to comprehend everything about each passage, but rather for you to understand what a variety of passages from different books of the Bible reveals about the topic of each study.

Threshold Bible Study offers you an opportunity to explore the entire Bible from the viewpoint of a variety of different themes. The commentary that follows each biblical passage launches your reflection about that passage and helps you begin to see its significance within the context of your contemporary experience. The questions following the commentary challenge you to understand the passage more fully and apply it to your own life. The prayer starter helps conclude your study by integrating learning into your relationship with God.

These studies are designed for maximum flexibility. Each study is presented in a workbook format, with sections for reading, reflecting, writing, discussing, and praying. Space for writing after each question is ideal for personal study and allows group members to prepare in advance for their discussion. The thirty lessons in each topic may be used by an individual over the period of a month, or by a group for six sessions, with lessons to be studied each week before the next group meeting. These studies are ideal for Bible study groups, small Christian communities, adult faith formation, student groups, Sunday school, neighborhood groups, and family reading, as well as for individual learning.

The method of Threshold Bible Study is rooted in the classical tradition of *lectio divina*, an ancient yet contemporary means for reading the Scriptures reflectively and prayerfully. Reading and interpreting the text (*lectio*) is followed by reflective meditation on its message (*meditatio*). This reading and reflecting flows into prayer from the heart (*oratio* and *contemplatio*).

This ancient method assures us that Bible study is a matter of both the mind and the heart. It is not just an intellectual exercise to learn more and be able to discuss the Bible with others. It is, more importantly, a transforming experience. Reflecting on God's word, guided by the Holy Spirit, illumines the mind with wisdom and stirs the heart with zeal.

Following the personal Bible study, Threshold Bible Study offers a method for extending *lectio divina* into a weekly conversation with a small group. This communal experience will allow participants to enhance their appreciation of the message and build up a spiritual community (*collatio*). The end result will be to increase not only individual faith, but also faithful witness in the context of daily life (*operatio*).

Through the spiritual disciplines of Scripture reading, study, reflection, conversation, and prayer, you will experience God's grace more abundantly as your life is rooted more deeply in Christ. The risen Jesus said: "Listen! I am standing at the door, knocking; if you hear my voice and open the door, I will come in to you and eat with you, and you with me" (Rev 3:20). Listen to the Word of God, open the door, and cross the threshold to an unimaginable dwelling with God!

SUGGESTIONS FOR INDIVIDUAL STUDY

• Make your Bible reading a time of prayer. Ask for God's guidance as your read the Scriptures.

• Try to study daily, or as often as possible according to the circumstances of your life.

• Read the Bible passage carefully, trying to understand both its meaning and its personal application as you read. Some persons find it helpful to read the passage aloud.

• Read the passage in another Bible translation. Each version adds to your understanding of the original text.

• Allow the commentary to help you comprehend and apply the scriptural text. The commentary is only a beginning, not the last word on the meaning of the passage.

• After reflecting on each question, write out your responses. The very act of writing will help you clarify your thoughts, bring new insights, and amplify your understanding.

• As you reflect on your answers, think about how you can live God's word in the context of your daily life.

• Conclude each daily lesson by reading the prayer and continuing with your own prayer from the heart.

• Make sure your reflections and prayers are matters of both the mind and the heart. A true encounter with God's word is always a transforming experience.

• Choose a word or a phrase from the lesson to carry with you throughout the day as a reminder of your encounter with God's life-changing word.

• Share your learning experience with at least one other person whom you trust for additional insights and affirmation. The ideal way to share learning is in a small group that meets regularly.

SUGGESTIONS FOR GROUP STUDY

• Meet regularly; weekly is ideal. Try to be on time and make attendance a high priority for the sake of the group. The average group meets for about an hour.

• Open each session with a prepared prayer, a song, or a reflection. Find some appropriate way to bring the group from the workaday world into a sacred time of graced sharing.

• If you have not been together before, name tags are very helpful as a group begins to become acquainted with the other group members.

• Spend the first session getting acquainted with one another, reading the Introduction aloud, and discussing the questions that follow.

• Appoint a group facilitator to provide guidance to the discussion. The role of facilitator may rotate among members each week. The facilitator simply keeps the discussion on track; each person shares responsibility for the group. There is no need for the facilitator to be a trained teacher.

• Try to study the six lessons on your own during the week. When you have done your own reflection and written your own answers, you will be better prepared to discuss the six scriptural lessons with the group. If you have not had an opportunity to study the passages during the week, meet with the group anyway to share support and insights.

• Participate in the discussion as much as you are able, offering your thoughts, insights, feelings, and decisions. You learn by sharing with others the fruits of your study.

• Be careful not to dominate the discussion. It is important that everyone in the group be offered an equal opportunity to share the results of their work. Try to link what you say to the comments of others so that the group remains on the topic.

• When discussing your own personal thoughts or feelings, use "I" language. Be as personal and honest as appropriate and be very cautious about giving advice to others.

• Listen attentively to the other members of the group so as to learn from their insights. The words of the Bible affect each person in a different way, so a group provides a wealth of understanding for each member.

• Don't fear silence. Silence in a group is as important as silence in personal study. It allows individuals time to listen to the voice of God's Spirit and the opportunity to form their thoughts before they speak.

• Solicit several responses for each question. The thoughts of different people will build on the answers of others and will lead to deeper insights for all.

• Don't fear controversy. Differences of opinions are a sign of a healthy and honest group. If you cannot resolve an issue, continue on, agreeing to disagree. There is probably some truth in each viewpoint.

• Discuss the questions that seem most important for the group. There is no need to cover all the questions in the group session.

• Realize that some questions about the Bible cannot be resolved, even by experts. Don't get stuck on some issue for which there are no clear answers.

• Whatever is said in the group is said in confidence and should be regarded as such.

• Pray as a group in whatever way feels comfortable. Pray for the members of your group throughout the week.

Schedule for group study

Session 1: Introduction   Date _____

Session 2: Lessons 1–6   Date _____

Session 3: Lessons 7–12   Date _____

Session 4: Lessons 13–18   Date _____

Session 5: Lessons 19–24   Date _____

Session 6: Lessons 25–30   Date _____

The Lord Jesus Christ will transform the body of our humiliation so that it may be conformed to the body of his glory. Phil 3:21

The Resurrection and the Life

Christians are a people with good news to share, and the font and pinnacle of that good news is the resurrection of Jesus Christ. Without the resurrection there would be no good news, no Christianity, no church. The resurrection is written in one way or another on every page of the New Testament. It is the belief that empowered the church at its beginning and that has sustained the church through the ages. If Christians ever stop believing in and living from the Lord's resurrection, that will be when the church stops being the church of Jesus Christ.

There is no reason why the joyous certainty of the early church in the resurrection of Christ should not be shared by the church today. It is the spark that set the disciples on fire. The simple followers of Jesus, saddened to death by the crucifixion of their master outside the wall of Jerusalem, were transformed within a short period of time into a jubilant community of believers. They proclaimed that the tomb was empty and that they had seen Jesus, alive again. The only real explanation for this remarkable series of events is that Jesus Christ had really been raised from the dead. It is the burning flame of that truth, the truth that he is truly risen, that can ignite people again with the good news capable of changing the world.

1

Reflection and discussion

• What thoughts and emotions come to mind in association with resurrection?

• Why does my life need good news? What could good news do for the world?

Beginning of the New Creation

Resurrection does not just describe what happened to Jesus after his death and burial. Resurrection is a past event, a future prospect, and a present reality. Our salvation is based on what God has done for us in human history, and the peak of that history of salvation was reached in Christ's resurrection from the dead. But since Jesus is still risen and alive, the resurrection transforms everything God's people will experience in the future and forms the guarantee of what God has promised for the end of time.

Jesus was the first in the human family to be raised and glorified. His resurrection proclaims a glorious hope for all creation: "Death has been swallowed up in victory" (1 Cor 15:54). We await the day when God will wipe away every tear (Rev 21:4). In him the new creation, promised for the end of the age, has begun. We see in him what God has promised as our destiny—resurrection from the dead and the fullness of life forever.

Most of the Greek world at the time of Jesus believed in the immortality of the soul, that a spiritual aspect of the human person was imprisoned within a mortal body and would be released at death. But Christianity teaches that the risen body of Christ is the archetype for the new humanity of the future.

We will be raised as whole, bodily persons, the same persons as before, with every aspect of life that makes us fully alive retained and perfected. Though dead and physically corrupted, we will be recalled to life by a new act of creation by God on the last day.

God loves all of his creation, and God does not abandon the bodies he has given us. In the resurrection of the dead, the nature of God as Creator and Redeemer becomes one. The natural order of our lives now will be transformed into a supernatural way of life. All the weaknesses and limitations of our present lives will be left behind. Our risen lives of glory will be more real, more vibrant, more alive than ever. The "seed" of our present lives will become the "fruit" of our resurrected lives.

Yet, the resurrection of Jesus is not just good news for our future. In his resurrection the future has already invaded the present. Death can already be mocked as a defeated enemy: "Where, O death, is your sting?" (1 Cor 15:55). The time of forgiveness, restoration, and victory over sin and death, promised by Israel's prophets and sages for the age to come, has already come upon the earth through Christ's resurrection. We can draw upon the resources of his power and grace in the here and now. His resurrection offers us a power for living to overcome even the most difficult obstacles and a purpose for living that assures us that what we do is not in vain.

We live our present lives in the interval between Christ's resurrection and the day of Christ's coming when the dead will be raised to life. We live now with a mixture of fulfillment and expectation. Jesus Christ is risen; he is alive forever. We can experience his risen presence in countless ways. Yet we await with eager longing for the fulfillment of the hope he has given us, the fullness of life in God's new creation.

Reflection and discussion

• In what ways do I experience the risen presence of Jesus in my life here and now?

• How does the resurrection inspire me to hope in the future?

The Revolutionary Doctrine of Resurrection

The resurrection—like the cross—is profoundly subversive of the values of the world. Contrary to the way the world views Easter—as a festive holiday legitimating a comfortable, culturally conventional religion—the central doctrine of Christianity is an explosive truth capable of bursting through the sealed tombs and locked doors of society's status quo. In raising Jesus from the dead, God reclaimed creation as his own, after sin, death, and the tragedies of worldly empires had done their destruction. Fiercely opposed by Sadducees and Caesars alike in the first century, the doctrine of resurrection proclaims to the rulers and nobles of this world allegiance to a different sovereign, a singular Lord.

In raising Jesus from the dead, God has seemingly done the impossible. Critics and skeptics through the ages have gone to great lengths in attempting to disprove and ridicule this core of Christian belief. But if the resurrection really happened, it matters profoundly. It made the world a different place and has given us the possibility of becoming a different kind of people. We cannot accept that Jesus Christ was bodily raised from the dead without becoming personally involved in the consequences of that reality.

Resurrection is God's ultimate affirmation that creation matters, that embodied human beings matter. God really does love these flawed, weak, and mortal bodies of ours. So what we do with our bodies and with the bodies of others is of ultimate significance in God's eyes. The bodily life of every person is supremely important and infinitely worthwhile. Resurrection spirituality is not an escape from creation; it is an intense participation in creation. It implies commitment to discipleship and to the worldwide mission Jesus' resurrection launched by inaugurating God's new age.

The resurrection does not just change our belief. It offers us a hope that changes the pattern of our living. Does it matter how we relate to one another—whether we are compassionate, honest, reliable, or generous? If this life were the be-all and end-all, maybe not. But since our lives are charged with the risen life of Christ, our existence is given new purpose and ultimate meaning. Everything we do has eternal significance, and nothing we do in the name of Christ is ever lost or wasted.

Reflection and discussion

• Why is the truth of resurrection so explosive and subversive?

• What does the resurrection commit me to in this world?

Describing an Awesome Mystery

All of the gospels describe the finding of the empty tomb and the first appearances of the risen Jesus as occurring in the early morning hours of the first day of the week. The Sabbath was the seventh day of the week for Judaism. The Lord's Day, the day of resurrection, was the first day, the day God's original creation started, and thus the opening day of God's new creation.

The first day of the week became the day on which Christians would gather for worship and Eucharist. While there was an annual celebration of Easter, the proclamation of Christ's resurrection was never limited to one day a year.

Rather, every Sunday became a little Easter, a celebration of the risen Christ and of the hope we share to be raised with him.

Adoration and worship is the best way to respond to the resurrection. Sacramental symbols, musical praise, and silent homage often convey better than words the truths of this awesome mystery. Human language fails us when trying to describe the risen life. It is like trying to describe a full moon over a white-capped ocean tide to a person born blind, or the magnificence of Beethoven's Ninth Symphony to a person who is congenitally deaf. What we will experience in the resurrection is so far beyond what we experience in this life that no words suffice.

The biblical writings challenge us to expand our imagination as they seek to express in human language something we have never experienced. The idea of resurrection is mostly absent from the Old Testament. Only a few passages from its later writings hint at the idea of bodily life after death. But in the New Testament, resurrection permeates its every stratum. Writers struggled to express in human language the reality of Christ's resurrection and the fullness of life we will one day share with him. After reviewing some of the key Old Testament passages, this study will look at the unique contribution of each New Testament author. We begin with Paul's letters and follow with the writings of each of the evangelists. Each writer has a different emphasis and different points to make. But each contributes to the kaleidoscope that is the biblical message of resurrection.

Reflection and discussion

• What have I experienced that is beyond the ability of my words to describe?

• How do I expect to be changed after this study?

Prayer

God of Glory, you have always called your people out of bondage and darkness. You have planted within us a longing for freedom and the fullness of life. Through the resurrection of your Son, you have given the world a reason to hope, and you have begun to create the whole world anew with glory. As I reflect on the explosive truth of the resurrection, help me know that your creation and the bodily lives of your people are supremely important in your eyes. Make me realize that nothing I do is ever lost or wasted when done in union with your Son, our Risen Lord.

SUGGESTIONS FOR FACILITATORS, GROUP SESSION 1

1. If the group is meeting for the first time, or if there are newcomers joining the group, it is helpful to provide nametags.

2. Ask the participants to introduce themselves and tell the group a bit about themselves. You may want to ask one or more of these introductory questions:
   - What drew you to join this group?
   - What is your biggest fear in beginning this Bible study?
   - How is beginning this study like a "threshold" for you?

3. Distribute the books to the members of the group.

4. You may want to pray this prayer as a group:

Come upon us, Holy Spirit, to enlighten and guide us as we begin this study of the resurrection. You inspired the writers of the Scriptures to proclaim the resurrection of Christ and our victory over death. Now stir our minds and our hearts to penetrate the truth of the resurrection and the eternal life we have been given through Christ. Motivate us to read the Scriptures, give us a love for God's word, and renew our lives and our hope through this study of the resurrection. Bless us during this session and throughout the coming week with the fire of your love.

5. Read the Introduction aloud, pausing at each question for discussion. Group members may wish to write the insights of the group as each question is discussed. Encourage several members of the group to respond to each question.

6. Don't feel compelled to finish the complete Introduction during the session. It is better to allow sufficient time to talk about the questions raised than to rush to the end. Group members may read any remaining sections on their own after the group meeting.

7. Instruct group members to read the first six lessons on their own during the six days before the next group meeting. They should write out their own answers to the questions as preparation for next week's group discussion.

8. Fill in the date for each group meeting under "Schedule for Group Study."

9. Conclude by praying aloud together the prayer at the end of the Introduction.

For everything there is a season, and a time for every matter under heaven: a time to be born, and a time to die. Eccl 3:1–2

To Dust You Shall Return

ECCLESIASTES 3:9–20 ⁹*What gain have the workers from their toil?* ¹⁰*I have seen the business that God has given to everyone to be busy with.* ¹¹*He has made everything suitable for its time; moreover he has put a sense of past and future into their minds, yet they cannot find out what God has done from the beginning to the end.* ¹²*I know that there is nothing better for them than to be happy and enjoy themselves as long as they live;* ¹³*moreover, it is God's gift that all should eat and drink and take pleasure in all their toil.* ¹⁴*I know that whatever God does endures forever; nothing can be added to it, nor anything taken from it; God has done this, so that all should stand in awe before him.* ¹⁵*That which is, already has been; that which is to be, already is; and God seeks out what has gone by.*

¹⁶*Moreover I saw under the sun that in the place of justice, wickedness was there, and in the place of righteousness, wickedness was there as well.* ¹⁷*I said in my heart, God will judge the righteous and the wicked, for he has appointed a time for every matter, and for every work.* ¹⁸*I said in my heart with regard to human beings that God is testing them to show that they are but animals.* ¹⁹*For the fate of humans and the fate of animals is the same; as one dies, so dies the other. They all have the same breath, and humans have no advantage over the animals; for all is vanity.* ²⁰*All go to one place; all are from the dust, and all turn to dust again.*

The book of Ecclesiastes contains the reflections of a Jewish sage who calls himself Qoheleth. He is constantly probing and asking questions of life. And after reviewing all the things that are often thought to make people happy—wealth, knowledge, accomplishments—he comes to the conclusion that nothing in life brings lasting satisfaction. The recurring theme of the book is the futility and emptiness of all that we do: "Vanity of vanities, all is vanity."

We work all our life and what do we have to show for it (verse 9)? We can't accomplish anything that is truly enduring or gainful in a lasting way. The wise person and the fool, the just person and the wicked, they all end up in the grave. Since life seems to have no permanence, it is simply a series of oscillating actions and reactions. Everything has its appropriate season and time in the rhythm of life's pendulum, which ultimately swings for each person from "a time to be born" to "a time to die" (3:2). Concerning every event of our lives, we can only know for certain that "this too shall pass."

Human beings have the capacity to look beyond the immediacy of life; God has put "a sense of past and future into their minds" (verse 11). Yet they are unable to discern the meaning of it all, to perceive a plan or direction that underlies the totality, "from the beginning to the end." According to Qoheleth, a sense of ultimate purposefulness and progression in life is utterly beyond human grasp.

Because the future is unknowable, much less controllable, the sage recommends a focus on the values of the present. "There is nothing better for them," he says, "than to be happy and enjoy themselves as long as they live" (verse 12). This ancient *carpe diem* is no hedonistic "eat, drink, and be merry." The sage, rather, is exhorting his listeners to appreciate and to be grateful for the simple pleasures of a good meal and a good day's work (verse 13). For better or for worse, that's as good as it gets since nothing else in life is certain or secure except what we experience in the moment.

The common fate of death undercuts any essential distinction between human beings and the animals (verse 19). All living beings share the life-breath which comes from God (see Gen 2:7), and when that breath is withdrawn, all creatures return to the ground from which they came. Qoheleth expresses life's ultimate futility by paraphrasing the words of God to Adam while explaining the consequences of Paradise lost: "You are dust, and to dust you shall return" (verse 20; Gen 3:19).

The reflections of Qoheleth are unsettling and troubling, sometimes even shocking, to the person of faith. Yet the author maintains the utmost reverence toward God. He always asserts that God is good, just, and wise; but he claims that we cannot understand the meaning of God's work. There is no lasting, secure happiness in life because we cannot discern a purposeful direction or goal. He concludes that this life, with all of its wonders and pleasures, cannot satisfy the longings of the human heart.

We've all felt like Qoheleth at times; we've felt discouraged, confused, and hopeless about life. When we realize that nothing in this world is lasting, it forces us to raise the same unsettling questions: Is life really worthwhile? Does life hold any lasting purpose or meaning? Does life really end in the dust of the grave? In Ecclesiastes there is no real resolution. It is essentially a book of questions waiting for answers.

Reflection and discussion

• Which of the ponderings of Qoheleth resonate most with me?

Animals end up in heaven too.

• What can the writer's pessimism about life's ultimate purpose teach me about the value of living each day to the full?

fearful of death and dieing is you don't believe in Jesus Christ our savior — that gave us eternal life.

"This too shall pass"

• What do the Ash Wednesday words, "You are dust, and to dust you shall return," teach me about life?

— Each day is a gift
focus on life and not death
each day god provides
blessings

• What are the advantages and disadvantages of having "a sense of past and future" in our minds?

God calls us to live in present
Learn to appreciate present
past is a great reference for the future.

• Since Ecclesiastes raises more questions than it offers answers, where do I search for a resolution to Qoheleth's dilemma?

New Testament

Prayer

Loving Creator, you have formed me from the dust of the earth and loaned me the breath of your life. As I live out the days of my life, give me glimpses of your plan for me so that I may live with purpose and hope.

I am like those who have no help, like those forsaken among the dead,
like the slain that lie in the grave, like those whom you remember no more.

Ps 88:4–5

The Desolation of the Grave

PSALM 88

¹*O Lord, God of my salvation,*
    when, at night, I cry out in your presence,
²*let my prayer come before you;*
    incline your ear to my cry.

³*For my soul is full of troubles,*
    and my life draws near to Sheol.
⁴*I am counted among those who go down to the Pit;*
    I am like those who have no help,
⁵*like those forsaken among the dead,*
    like the slain that lie in the grave,
like those whom you remember no more,
    for they are cut off from your hand.
⁶*You have put me in the depths of the Pit,*
    in the regions dark and deep.
⁷*Your wrath lies heavy upon me,*
    and you overwhelm me with all your waves. Selah

⁸*You have caused my companions to shun me;*
  you have made me a thing of horror to them.
I am shut in so that I cannot escape;
  ⁹*my eye grows dim through sorrow.*
Every day I call on you, O Lord;
  I spread out my hands to you.
¹⁰*Do you work wonders for the dead?*
  Do the shades rise up to praise you? Selah
¹¹*Is your steadfast love declared in the grave,*
  or your faithfulness in Abaddon?
¹²*Are your wonders known in the darkness,*
  or your saving help in the land of forgetfulness?

¹³*But I, O Lord, cry out to you;*
  in the morning my prayer comes before you.
¹⁴*O Lord, why do you cast me off?*
  Why do you hide your face from me?
¹⁵*Wretched and close to death from my youth up,*
  I suffer your terrors; I am desperate.
¹⁶*Your wrath has swept over me;*
  your dread assaults destroy me.
¹⁷*They surround me like a flood all day long;*
  from all sides they close in on me.
¹⁸*You have caused friend and neighbor to shun me;*
  my companions are in darkness.

This psalm of lament is the gloomiest in the psalter. The singer prays to God in great distress while at the point of death. Intense physical and emotional pain engulf the singer as darkness and death are closing in. The lament speaks not only of the pain that leads to death, but of death itself. *dark*

The psalm starkly but accurately portrays the Israelites' bleak view of death throughout most of the Old Testament. Death is the threshold of the abyss, going down to the Pit, drowning in God's wrath, shunned by companions. The realm of the dead was thought of simply as an extension of the grave. Its

Hebrew name was Sheol, the netherworld, or Abaddon, the place of perishing. It is a negation of every characteristic of life. Sheol is murky, unrelenting darkness and silence, the land of the forgotten. God's presence does not reach there; the dead are cut off from God's memory and providence. The answer to each of the bitter questions in verses 10–12 is *no.*

The diversity of images that depict death and dying express the horror felt by the ancient Israelite at the prospect of death. Approaching the grave is likened to going down into a deep pit. The metaphor suggests the image of a cistern, a place dark and mucky, with no means of escape (verses 6, 8). Dying feels like drowning, surrounded as in a flood and swept over and overwhelmed by waves (verses 7, 16–17). The psychological anguish is exhausting: eyes dimmed with sorrow (verse 9), feeling wretched, terrorized, and desperate (verse 15).

Most terrible for the Israelite is the total separation from God. The dead are forsaken, no longer remembered by God, cut off from God's care (verse 5). They are no longer able to offer praise to God, and God ceases to perform saving wonders beyond the boundaries of death (verse 10–12). The dark, lonely realm of death is truly the "land of forgetfulness."

The mystery that penetrates this psalm is the singer's rhetorical questions: "Why do you cast me off? Why do you hide your face from me?" (verse 14). Thy dying person cries out to God, morning and night (verses 1, 9, 13). Why should the "God of my salvation" deny deliverance to the one who prays in the anguish of death? The "why" of the psalmist is the springboard for further searching into the mystery of God's plan.

Reflection and discussion

• What are the images and metaphors for death scattered throughout the psalm?

- Have I ever experienced the silence of God and the darkness of death?

- Are there any glimmers of hope in this psalm of lament?

- Why do the questions of verses 10–12 demand answers from God's further revelation?

because there is doubt in death

Prayer

> *God of my salvation, you give life and take it back again. When I am on the verge of death, do not hide your face from me, but be near me with your comforting presence. Help me trust in your word and hope in your promises.*

"I will lay sinews on you, and will cause flesh to come upon you, and cover you with skin, and put breath in you, and you shall live." Ezek 37:6

Can These Dry Bones Live?

EZEKIEL 37:1–14 ¹*The hand of the Lord came upon me, and he brought me out by the spirit of the Lord and set me down in the middle of a valley; it was full of bones.* ²*He led me all around them; there were very many lying in the valley, and they were very dry.* ³*He said to me, "Mortal, can these bones live?" I answered, "O Lord God, you know."* ⁴*Then he said to me, "Prophesy to these bones, and say to them: O dry bones, hear the word of the Lord.* ⁵*Thus says the Lord God to these bones: I will cause breath to enter you, and you shall live.* ⁶*I will lay sinews on you, and will cause flesh to come upon you, and cover you with skin, and put breath in you, and you shall live; and you shall know that I am the Lord."*

⁷*So I prophesied as I had been commanded; and as I prophesied, suddenly there was a noise, a rattling, and the bones came together, bone to its bone.* ⁸*I looked, and there were sinews on them, and flesh had come upon them, and skin had covered them; but there was no breath in them.* ⁹*Then he said to me, "Prophesy to the breath, prophesy, mortal, and say to the breath: Thus says the Lord God: Come from the four winds, O breath, and breathe upon these slain, that they may live."* ¹⁰*I prophesied as he commanded me, and the breath came into them, and they lived, and stood on their feet, a vast multitude.*

¹¹*Then he said to me, "Mortal, these bones are the whole house of Israel. They say, 'Our bones are dried up, and our hope is lost; we are cut off completely.'*

¹²Therefore prophesy, and say to them, Thus says the Lord God: I am going to open your graves, and bring you up from your graves, O my people; and I will bring you back to the land of Israel. ¹³And you shall know that I am the Lord, when I open your graves, and bring you up from your graves, O my people. ¹⁴I will put my spirit within you, and you shall live, and I will place you on your own soil; then you shall know that I, the Lord, have spoken and will act," says the Lord.

The prophet Ezekiel's visionary experience brought him to a valley filled with a great number of dry bones strewn loosely on the ground (verses 1–2). God tells Ezekiel his intention to cover the bones with sinew, flesh, and skin, and to put in them the breath of new life. God then carries out his intention through the word of his prophet. The result of Ezekiel's prophesying, with a noise and a rattling, is accomplished in two stages. The first is the joining of the bones into skeletons and the covering with sinews, flesh, and skin (verses 7–8). Only then does Ezekiel prophesy to the life-giving breath which comes into the corpses to make them live (verses 9–10).

The narrative is held together by the key Hebrew word, *ruah*. It occurs ten times and can be translated "spirit," "breath," or "wind." The scene is a reenactment of the primal act of creation, when the spirit/breath/wind of God swept over the waters of chaos to infuse life into an inert universe (Gen 1:2), and when God formed humanity from the dust of the ground and breathed into its nostrils the breath/spirit of life (Gen 2:7). That same *ruah* of God caused the valley of bones to become a vast, living multitude (verse 10).

The vision is interpreted as an oracle of hope and restoration. The dry bones are the people of Israel in exile: broken in spirit, bereft of hope, cut off from their source of life (verse 11). But God would raise the Israelite nation from their graves and give them new life again as a people, living once again in their own land (verse 12). It is God's spirit who animates them, regathers them as a people, and gives them the will to accept their future (verse 14).

Though this prophecy was written before Israel came to believe in personal life after death, the passage was interpreted by later Jewish and Christian writers as a prophecy of individual resurrection from death. The God who faithfully brought his people from death to life is the God who will be faithful even beyond the grave, giving life back to those who have died.

Reflection and discussion

• What are the two stages in the restoration of the dry bones to life? What do these stages express?

Our brokeness in death is then healed through Christ's salvation.

• How is the Hebrew word *ruah* used in various senses in this passage (verses 5, 9, 14)?

spirit, breath, and wind

• How do I lift my spirit and hope? What can I do for those who feel they are but dry bones?

—go to church
—prayer
— be the light of Christ and spirit of god for them.

Prayer

Spirit of the Living God, come upon your people and give us renewed life. When we are broken in spirit and lacking in hope, breathe upon us and restore us. Help me believe that you are always faithful, in this life and beyond the grave.

**Your dead shall live, their corpses shall rise.
O dwellers in the dust, awake and sing for joy!** Isa 26:19

Sleepers in the Dust Shall Awake

ISAIAH 26:16–19

¹⁶*O Lord, in distress they sought you,*
  they poured out a prayer
  when your chastening was on them.
¹⁷*Like a woman with child,*
  who writhes and cries out in her pangs
  when she is near her time,
so were we because of you, O Lord;
  ¹⁸*we were with child, we writhed,*
  but we gave birth only to wind.
We have won no victories on earth,
  and no one is born to inhabit the world.
¹⁹*Your dead shall live, their corpses shall rise.*
  O dwellers in the dust, awake and sing for joy!
For your dew is a radiant dew,
  and the earth will give birth to those long dead.

DANIEL 12:1–4 ¹*"At that time Michael, the great prince, the protector of your people, shall arise. There shall be a time of anguish, such as has never occurred since nations first came into existence. But at that time your people shall be delivered, everyone who is found written in the book. ²Many of those who sleep in the dust of the earth shall awake, some to everlasting life, and some to shame and everlasting contempt. ³Those who are wise shall shine like the brightness of the sky, and those who lead many to righteousness, like the stars forever and ever. ⁴But you, Daniel, keep the words secret and the book sealed until the time of the end. Many shall be running back and forth, and evil shall increase."*

These writings from Israel's prophets are some of the earliest texts in the Bible to speak about resurrection. These prophetic texts speak about God's fidelity to his creation, especially to his people Israel, and about a bodily return to life for those who have died. Both Isaiah's "dwellers in the dust" and Daniel's "those who sleep in the dust of the earth" will "awake" (Isa 26:19; Dan 12:2). The fate of fallen humanity as expressed in Genesis, "to dust you shall return" (Gen 3:19), may not be the final word from a faithful God. The hope of individual resurrection is rooted in these ancient texts that express the restoration of God's people.

The passage from Isaiah is set in the context of a prayer for God's help against enemies. The speaker complains that Israel writhed like a woman in birthpangs but never received the joy of birth. God's people were in distress, but experienced no victories (Isa 26:17–18). But after lodging complaints, a voice breaks forth with a confident trust, convinced that those who have died will finally "awake and sing for joy" (Isa 26:19). The new birth of God's people includes individual resurrection for those who have died: "Your dead shall live, their corpses shall rise."

The verses from Daniel are likewise set within the context of crisis. The Jews were experiencing a period of terrible persecution. The prophet proclaims that, despite the coming "time of anguish," the faithful who are "written in the book" of life will be delivered (Dan 12:1). On that climactic day, Michael, the angel who protects God's people, will triumph. God will deliver his people from their persecutors and bring their distress to an end. In addition, many of those who have died will awake to "everlasting life"—the first occurrence of this term in the Bible (Dan 12:2). When the prophet says that "those who are wise" and "those who lead many to righteousness" will shine like the stars in the sky forever (Dan 12:3), he means that the risen ones will not simply return to life much as they knew it before. Rather they will be raised to a state of glory in the world comparable to the status of stars within creation.

Scholars debate whether these two passages promise individual resurrection or use resurrection as an image to speak about the restoration of Israel as a nation. Yet in reality the two meanings cannot be separated. These passages indicate that the idea of resurrection is always closely tied to the idea of the restoration of God's people. The rescue and revival of God's people includes the resurrection of the dead. Israel's hope for resurrection was first of all a hope for themselves as a community, not just for individuals. This emerging belief in the bodily resurrection, not yet mature in these two prophetic texts, would be fleshed out as the central teaching of the New Testament about the future.

The promise of resurrection is firmly linked to creation itself. God created his people from the dust of the earth and breathed into them his own breath. The fresh gift of his breath will bring the dust to life again. Though death was linked to expulsion from the garden in Genesis 3, the full restoration of God's people involves the new bodily creation of human beings after the state of death. At the resurrection of the dead, human beings will no longer be shadows lost in the darkness of Sheol, but will be re-created by God as bodies able to think, will, and feel—fully alive again in a regained paradise.

Reflection and discussion

• How do the images of birthpangs and childbirth help me to understand the suffering, purpose, and hope involved in a life of faith?

like a beautiful miracle waiting for us at the end.
— the new life comes after the struggle
— the pain goes away when the labor is over.

• What is similar in the thought of these two prophets?

Hope of restoration

— dead shall return to everlasting life

• What indicates that this embryonic belief in resurrection awaits its full development in the teachings of the New Testament?

the hope of resurrection
— Jesus is in the New Testament

• What most convinces me that God is faithful and will not abandon me in death?

— your dead shall live and your corpses shall rise.
God tells us that

Prayer

Eternal and faithful God, you never desire the work of your creative hand to undergo corruption. I know that you will never abandon me, and I look for the day when you will awaken my body to life everlasting.

For if he were not expecting that those who had fallen would rise again, it would have been superfluous and foolish to pray for the dead. 2 Macc 12:44

Expecting the Fallen to Rise Again

2 MACCABEES 7:20–23 ²⁰*The mother was especially admirable and worthy of honorable memory. Although she saw her seven sons perish within a single day, she bore it with good courage because of her hope in the Lord.* ²¹*She encouraged each of them in the language of their ancestors. Filled with a noble spirit, she reinforced her woman's reasoning with a man's courage, and said to them,* ²²*"I do not know how you came into being in my womb. It was not I who gave you life and breath, nor I who set in order the elements within each of you.* ²³*Therefore the Creator of the world, who shaped the beginning of humankind and devised the origin of all things, will in his mercy give life and breath back to you again, since you now forget yourselves for the sake of his laws."*

2 MACCABEES 12:39–45 ³⁹*On the next day, as had now become necessary, Judas and his men went to take up the bodies of the fallen and to bring them back to lie with their kindred in the sepulchers of their ancestors.* ⁴⁰*Then under the tunic of each one of the dead they found sacred tokens of the idols of Jamnia, which the law forbids the Jews to wear. And it became clear to all that this was the reason these men had fallen.* ⁴¹*So they all blessed the ways of the*

Lord, the righteous judge, who reveals the things that are hidden; [42]and they turned to supplication, praying that the sin that had been committed might be wholly blotted out. The noble Judas exhorted the people to keep themselves free from sin, for they had seen with their own eyes what had happened as the result of the sin of those who had fallen. [43]He also took up a collection, man by man, to the amount of two thousand drachmas of silver, and sent it to Jerusalem to provide for a sin-offering. In doing this he acted very well and honorably, taking account of the resurrection. [44]For if he were not expecting that those who had fallen would rise again, it would have been superfluous and foolish to pray for the dead. [45]But if he was looking to the splendid reward that is laid up for those who fall asleep in godliness, it was a holy and pious thought. Therefore he made atonement for the dead, so that they might be delivered from their sin.

The Greek ruler Antiochus Epiphanes tried to force Jews to give up the practices of their religion and adopt the ways of the Greek culture. The persecution described in 2 Maccabees took place around 168 B.C. In chapter 7, the centerpiece of the book, the writer recounts the story of seven brothers who were arrested along with their mother. When they refused to eat pork as the king demanded, he subjected the brothers to torture, one by one, in their mother's presence. Each of them remained faithful to God's law, despite their terrible suffering and death, strengthened by their belief that God would raise them back to life at some future date.

The valiant mother encouraged her sons with hope in the resurrection: "The Creator of the world, who shaped the beginning of humankind and devised the origin of all things, will in his mercy give life and breath back to you again" (7:23). The God who created each of her sons in her own womb will perform a mighty act of new creation in which the martyrs will be given new bodies and a new breath of life.

Further indication of belief in the resurrection is shown in chapter 12. The author indicates that Judas Maccabee believed that God would raise the dead to life since he ordered prayers and sacrifices for those who had fallen in battle. After discovering that those who had been killed by the enemy troops had been wearing idolatrous tokens under their cloaks, Judas concluded that this was the reason they had been slain (12:40). His response was to praise God for bringing their transgression to light, to pray that the sin might be blotted out, and to take up a collection so that a sin-offering could be made at the temple in Jerusalem (12:41–43). The writer notes that in doing these things, Judas "acted very well and honorably, taking account of the resurrection" (12:43). The reason for his actions was his belief that the fallen soldiers would rise from the dead: "For if he were not expecting that those who had fallen would rise again, it would have been superfluous and foolish to pray for the dead" (12:44).

The fallen soldiers needed to be forgiven of their sins so that, when the day of resurrection occurred, they could join with the martyrs and all the righteous. At death, according to the Jews of the Maccabee era, humans "fall asleep" (12:45), from which they awaken only on the day of the resurrection. Between their death and their future resurrection they are in a kind of intermediate state in which the prayers and sacrifices of the living can affect their forgiveness and purification.

Reflection and discussion

• What is the most difficult thing I have ever done in obedience to God's will?

when my personal agenda gets in the way of God's agenda

• What in these passages indicates a clear belief in the resurrection of the dead among the Jews in the Maccabee era?

Praying for dead.
The Woman's hope that

• How does the reasoning of a mother offer a unique insight into the future resurrection of her children?

— She was able to watch her sons be maimed but had faith. reinforced woman's reasoning w/ man's courage

• How does the collection taken up by Judas Maccabee indicate the Jewish belief in the resurrection of the dead?

• In what ways does the church today offer prayers and offerings for those who have died?

— Mass
— novenas
— honors saints
— petitions

Prayer

Loving Creator, you gave me life and breath in my mother's womb. Fill me with courage to do your will, despite the costs. Give me the confident hope that after my death you will give life and breath back to me again.

**They will govern nations and rule over peoples,
and the Lord will reign over them for ever.** Wis 3:8

God Watches Over
His Elect

WISDOM 2:21—3:9 ²¹*Thus they reasoned, but they were led astray,*
for their wickedness blinded them,
²²and they did not know the secret purposes of God,
nor hoped for the wages of holiness,
nor discerned the prize for blameless souls;
²³for God created us for incorruption,
and made us in the image of his own eternity,
²⁴but through the devil's envy death entered the world,
and those who belong to his company experience it.

3 ¹*But the souls of the righteous are in the hand of God,*
and no torment will ever touch them.
²In the eyes of the foolish they seemed to have died,
and their departure was thought to be a disaster,
³and their going from us to be their destruction;
but they are at peace.
⁴For though in the sight of others they were punished,

28

their hope is full of immortality.
⁵Having been disciplined a little, they will receive great good,
because God tested them and found them worthy of himself;
⁶like gold in the furnace he tried them,
and like a sacrificial burnt-offering he accepted them.
⁷In the time of their visitation they will shine forth,
and will run like sparks through the stubble.
⁸They will govern nations and rule over peoples,
and the Lord will reign over them for ever.
⁹Those who trust in him will understand truth,
and the faithful will abide with him in love,
because grace and mercy are upon his holy ones,
and he watches over his elect.

The book of Wisdom was the last book of the Old Testament to be written, probably just a few decades before the birth of Jesus. Though its Jewish writer wrote in Greek, the work shows its readers that true wisdom is found in God's revelation to Israel, not in the pagan ways of Greek culture. The sage describes the wicked as blind, unable to understand "the secret purposes of God" (2:21–22). In view of God's purposes, death is an intruder, entering the human condition because of sin, and those who follow the devil's company experience the full effects of death. The faithful, however, understand that God created us in his own immortal "image," designed for "incorruption" (2:23–24).

The sage reminds the readers that the foolish are mistaken when they view the death of the righteous as "disaster" and "destruction" (3:2–3). On the contrary, since God has made his people for everlasting life, those who have died are "at peace" and "their hope is full of immortality" (3:3–4). When death is assumed to be the end of life, suffering is presumed to be a punishment for some wrong action, as was commonly believed in earlier period's of Israel's history. But when death is acknowledged as only a passing into immortality, suffering can be recognized as a discipline, a testing of fidelity through which God recognizes those who are worthy of himself (3:5–6).

As the Jewish understanding of resurrection developed, it was natural that questions should arise concerning the state of those who had died as they await the great day of resurrection. Wisdom borrowed the Greek philosophical concept of the "soul" to designate that aspect of the human person that continues to live after death. The sage assures his readers that "the souls of the just are in the hand of God" (3:1). After the death of the corruptible body, the soul lives on, safely and peacefully in God's care until the glorious re-embodiment of resurrection.

The sage then goes on to describe the future state of resurrection for the righteous. "The time of their visitation" (3:7) is God's final judgment and victory. This new and ultimate stage of salvation in described with verbs in the future tense. God's righteous ones "will shine forth" in their renewed and glorious condition. Using prophetic language describing the restoration of Israel, the sage says that God's faithful will "govern nations and rule over peoples" and the reign of God over all creation will be experienced in its fullness (3:8). Those who trust God will understand God's truth, experience his mercy and grace, and live in his love forever (3:9).

Reflection and discussion

• How am I able to think about the meaning of suffering in a different way because of my hope of eternal life?

— that at some point in time there won't be suffering and pain anymore,
— preparation to be with God someday in Heaven

• In what way is death disastrous and destructive? What aspects of who I am are unable to be destroyed by death? Soul and Spirit.

Spirits of people do live on.

Bad for people left behind there is suffering.

• How does the book of Wisdom describe the state of those who have died as they await their future resurrection?

souls are in the hand of God, peace and hope

• What in this passage most convinces me that my life will never end?

Versus 8 - 9 and 23

• How does the teaching on resurrection differ in the later books of the Old Testament than in the earlier books?

It actually says there is resurrection. It gives hope later on,

Prayer

God of mercy and love, I know that you created me for eternity and made me ultimately incorruptible. Fill my life with hope for immortality and help me to trust in you. Watch over me in this life, and when my life is done, let me enter into your reign.

SUGGESTIONS FOR FACILITATORS, GROUP SESSION 2

1. If there are newcomers who were not present for the first group session, introduce them now.

2. You may want to pray this prayer as a group:

Faithful God, we know that when our earthly life is over we will return to the dust of the ground from which we came. Yet, we know through the Scriptures of our ancestors that you never abandon your people and that you will restore your faithful ones to life. You created us in your own immortal image and planted within us the hope of immortality. Bless us with your Holy Spirit as we study the Scriptures, give us a deeper trust in God's plan, and help us to know that God will create our bodies anew after death and raise us in glory on the last day.

3. Ask one or more of the following questions:
   - What was your biggest challenge in Bible study over this past week?
   - What did you learn about the Old Testament this week?

4. Discuss lessons 1 through 6 together. Assuming that group members have read the Scripture and commentary during the week, there is no need to read it aloud. As you review each lesson, you might want to briefly summarize the Scripture passage of each lesson and ask the group what struck them most from the commentary.

5. Choose one or more of the questions for reflection and discussion from each lesson to talk over as a group. You may want to ask group members which question was most challenging or helpful to them as you review each lesson.

6. Keep the discussion moving, but don't rush the discussion in order to complete more questions. Allow time for the questions that provoke the most discussion.

7. Remember that there are no definitive answers for these discussion questions. The insights of group members will add to the understanding of all. None of these questions requires an expert.

8. Instruct group members to complete lessons 7 through 12 on their own during the six days before the next group meeting. They should write out their own answers to the questions as preparation for next week's session.

9. Conclude by praying aloud together the prayer at the end of lesson 6, or any other prayer you choose.

I handed on to you as of first importance what I in turn had received:
that Christ died for our sins in accordance with the scriptures,
and that he was buried, and that he was raised on the third day
in accordance with the scriptures. 1 Cor 15:3–4

Holding Firmly to the Message of Resurrection

1 CORINTHIANS 15:1–11 ¹*Now I would remind you, brothers and sisters, of the good news that I proclaimed to you, which you in turn received, in which also you stand, ²through which also you are being saved, if you hold firmly to the message that I proclaimed to you—unless you have come to believe in vain.*

³For I handed on to you as of first importance what I in turn had received: that Christ died for our sins in accordance with the scriptures, ⁴and that he was buried, and that he was raised on the third day in accordance with the scriptures, ⁵and that he appeared to Cephas, then to the twelve. ⁶Then he appeared to more than five hundred brothers and sisters at one time, most of whom are still alive, though some have died. ⁷Then he appeared to James, then to all the apostles. ⁸Last of all, as to one untimely born, he appeared also to me. ⁹For I am the least of the apostles, unfit to be called an apostle, because I persecuted the church of God. ¹⁰But by the grace of God I am what I am, and his grace toward me has not been in vain. On the contrary, I worked harder than any of them—

though it was not I, but the grace of God that is with me. [11] *Whether then it was I or they, so we proclaim and so you have come to believe.*

The resurrection is at the heart of Paul's letters, and this chapter of 1 Corinthians is the most extended discussion on resurrection in the Bible. No longer was resurrection just a distant hope that most Jews shared; now it was the wondrous new reality that God had brought into the world by raising Jesus from the dead. The new glorious existence foretold by the prophets and sages of Israel, which was expected to occur in the final age, had suddenly, unexpectedly begun.

The heart of the gospel, what Paul received and handed on, is this: Christ died for our sins and was buried; Christ was raised from the dead and appeared to his disciples (verses 3–5). Paul says that this early statement of Christian belief is "of first importance." Here is the essence of the Christian faith in a nutshell.

This supremely important core of belief insists that Christ died and was raised "in accordance with the scriptures" (verses 3–4). Because there are no Old Testament texts that specifically anticipate the death or resurrection of the Messiah, most probably the emphasis is on the witness of the Old Testament as a whole: God's care for creation, fidelity to the covenant, unwavering love for his people, and his power over all opposing forces. Christ's saving death and glorious resurrection was not an afterthought, but was part and parcel of the divine plan. God's rescue of humanity from sin and death through Christ is the final phase of the story of salvation for ancient Israel.

The list of witnesses to the appearances of Christ is an indication that the resurrection was real (verses 5–7). Paul most certainly did not believe that the resurrection was simply an ineffable, subjective experience or hallucination. His enumeration of a large though finite number of witnesses, noting that most were still living, indicates that there was a convincing number willing to testify that they had seen Jesus alive.

Paul links his own witness to Christ's resurrection with the Lord's appearances to his original followers, yet Paul notes that his was "last of all" (verse 8). When Paul saw the risen Christ the appearances were at an end. In this way Paul distinguishes the appearances of the risen Christ from every later type of subjective vision and personal experience of Christ. He compares his own witness to "someone untimely born." He was not ready for his own new birth. The other witnesses had been able to prepare for the appearance of the risen Christ by keeping company with him during his early ministry. Paul did not. As a persecutor of the church, Paul was clearly unprepared for his own dazzling encounter with the glorious Lord (verses 9–10). Yet, God's transforming grace made him what he is for us and for Christ's church.

Reflection and discussion

• What verses in this passage indicate to me that the resurrection of Jesus is real?

• What is the primary difference between the Old and New Testament teachings on resurrection?

• Paul urges us to "hold firmly to the message." What in my life can sometimes cause me to loosen my grip on the gospel message?

Prayer

Father of Jesus, I am what I am through your grace. You raised Jesus from the death and caused him to be seen by his apostles and disciples. Give me a fresh experience of your merciful love today and help me to witness the goodness you have poured into my life through your Son.

**If Christ has not been raised, your faith is futile
and you are still in your sins.** 1 Cor 15:17

Made Alive in Christ

1 CORINTHIANS 15:12–28 *¹²Now if Christ is proclaimed as raised from
the dead, how can some of you say there is no resurrection of the dead? ¹³If there
is no resurrection of the dead, then Christ has not been raised; ¹⁴and if Christ
has not been raised, then our proclamation has been in vain and your faith has
been in vain. ¹⁵We are even found to be misrepresenting God, because we testi-
fied of God that he raised Christ—whom he did not raise if it is true that the
dead are not raised. ¹⁶For if the dead are not raised, then Christ has not been
raised. ¹⁷If Christ has not been raised, your faith is futile and you are still in
your sins. ¹⁸Then those also who have died in Christ have perished. ¹⁹If for this
life only we have hoped in Christ, we are of all people most to be pitied.*

*²⁰But in fact Christ has been raised from the dead, the first fruits of those who
have died. ²¹For since death came through a human being, the resurrection of
the dead has also come through a human being; ²²for as all die in Adam, so all
will be made alive in Christ. ²³But each in his own order: Christ the first fruits,
then at his coming those who belong to Christ. ²⁴Then comes the end, when he
hands over the kingdom to God the Father, after he has destroyed every ruler
and every authority and power. ²⁵For he must reign until he has put all his
enemies under his feet. ²⁶The last enemy to be destroyed is death. ²⁷For "God has
put all things in subjection under his feet." But when it says, "All things are put*

in subjection," it is plain that this does not include the one who put all things in subjection under him. ²⁸*When all things are subjected to him, then the Son himself will also be subjected to the one who put all things in subjection under him, so that God may be all in all.*

P aul now tells us the reason for his extended discussion of the resurrection: Some of the Corinthians were saying there is no resurrection of the dead (verse 12). Apparently some of the community believed only in continuing life after death through the survival of the soul, but not through an act of new creation by God in the resurrection of the dead. This dualistic understanding of the human person—an immortal soul imprisoned within a body that dies and corrupts—was the Greek view that dominated most of the ancient world. Paul insists that the whole human person, created by God, will be given a new, transformed bodily life through the resurrection of the dead.

Paul develops his argument gently and thoroughly. If there is no resurrection of the dead, then Christ cannot have been raised, because he was dead (verses 13, 16). And if Christ has not been raised, then the apostles have been talking empty nonsense, and those who believed them have believed empty nonsense (verses 14, 17). In which case, Christians are liars who misrepresent God (verse 15), there is no forgiveness of sins (verse 17), and those who have died as Christians are simply lost (verse 18). The Christian gospel stands or falls with the resurrection of the dead. Without the resurrection, Christianity is only a system of delusions and futile human fantasy, leaving its adherents "most to be pitied" (verse 19).

Sweeping away all the gloomy hypothetical consequences that follow from denying the resurrection, Paul triumphantly declares: "But in fact Christ has been raised from the dead" (verse 20). As a Jew, Paul had expected the resurrection to be a corporate raising of all God's people at a future time that God would determine. To claim that only Jesus was raised from the dead, before all others and before the end of the age, seemed to go against the biblical expectation. Paul therefore uses the metaphor of the "first fruits," the first sheaf of the grain harvest waved at the Jewish Feast of Weeks as a sign and promise of the remainder of the harvest to come. By calling the risen Christ the "first fruits of those who have died," Paul indicates that he understood the resurrection of Christ as an anticipatory promise of the general resurrection of the dead (verses 20, 24).

Just as Adam is a representational figure of failed humanity, the risen Christ represents renewed, resurrected humanity. Through Adam, death came into the world; through Christ will come the resurrection of the dead (verses 21–22). Paul portrays salvation as a great drama in which Christ gains victory over all the forces arrayed in opposition to God. The "last enemy" to be subdued by Christ is death itself (verse 24–26). In the resurrection of Christ, death's fate is sealed, but death is still active in creation until its final defeat. Then at the end, all who belong to Christ will be raised to life again, and Christ will hand over the kingdom to the Father so that God alone will be sovereign over all creation (verses 24, 28).

We live now in the interval between Christ's resurrection and the day of Christ's coming when the dead will be raised to life. The time of forgiveness, restoration, and victory over sin and death, promised by Israel's prophets and sages for the age to come, has already come upon the earth through the resurrection of Christ. The future age has already burst into the present age, so that we live now with a mixture of fulfillment and expectation. What happened when Christ rose from the tomb has made the world a different place, and has given us the possibility to become a different kind of people.

Reflection and discussion

• Why is the resurrection of Jesus the bedrock of Christianity?

• What is the difference between the soul's life after death and the resurrection of the dead?

• How does the image of the "first fruits" indicate the relationship of Christ's resurrection to our own?

• Why does Paul call death an enemy? What assurance do I have that death will not have the last word?

• In what way is the present age a time of both fulfillment and expectation?

Prayer

Risen Christ, you are raised from the dead; you are my hope of resurrection. Without you I am trapped in sin and destined for eternal death. Because of you death's fate is sealed and I can live in joyful hope.

The trumpet will sound, and the dead will be raised imperishable, and we will be changed. For this perishable body must put on imperishability, and this mortal body must put on immortality.

1 Cor 15:52–53

Where, O Death, Is Your Victory?

1 COR 15:35–58 *35But someone will ask, "How are the dead raised? With what kind of body do they come?" 36Fool! What you sow does not come to life unless it dies. 37And as for what you sow, you do not sow the body that is to be, but a bare seed, perhaps of wheat or of some other grain. 38But God gives it a body as he has chosen, and to each kind of seed its own body. 39Not all flesh is alike, but there is one flesh for human beings, another for animals, another for birds, and another for fish. 40There are both heavenly bodies and earthly bodies, but the glory of the heavenly is one thing, and that of the earthly is another. 41There is one glory of the sun, and another glory of the moon, and another glory of the stars; indeed, star differs from star in glory. 42So it is with the resurrection of the dead. What is sown is perishable, what is raised is imperishable. 43It is sown in dishonor, it is raised in glory. It is sown in weakness, it is raised in power. 44It is sown a physical body, it is raised a spiritual body. If there is a physical body, there is also a spiritual body. 45Thus it is written, "The first man, Adam, became a living being"; the last Adam became a life-giving spirit. 46But* *it is not the spiritual that is first, but the physical, and then the spiritual. ⁴⁷The first man was from the earth, a man of dust; the second man is from heaven. ⁴⁸As was the man of dust, so are those who are of the dust; and as is the man of heaven, so are those who are of heaven. ⁴⁹Just as we have borne the image of the man of dust, we will also bear the image of the man of heaven.*

⁵⁰What I am saying, brothers and sisters, is this: flesh and blood cannot inherit the kingdom of God, nor does the perishable inherit the imperishable. ⁵¹ Listen, I will tell you a mystery! We will not all die, but we will all be changed, ⁵²in a moment, in the twinkling of an eye, at the last trumpet. For the trumpet will sound, and the dead will be raised imperishable, and we will be changed. ⁵³For this perishable body must put on imperishability, and this mortal body must put on immortality. ⁵⁴When this perishable body puts on imperishability, and this mortal body puts on immortality, then the saying that is written will be fulfilled: "Death has been swallowed up in victory." ⁵⁵ "Where, O death, is your victory? Where, O death, is your sting?" ⁵⁶The sting of death is sin, and the power of sin is the law. ⁵⁷But thanks be to God, who gives us the victory through our Lord Jesus Christ.

⁵⁸Therefore, my beloved, be steadfast, immovable, always excelling in the work of the Lord, because you know that in the Lord your labor is not in vain.

Because resurrection is far beyond anything we have ever experienced or anything we can fully comprehend, we ask questions much like those addressed to Paul: "How are the dead raised? With what kind of body do they come?" (verse 35). Because human language is incapable of adequately expressing the reality of resurrection, Paul turns to metaphors and analogies to help his hearers understand. The Corinthians naively assumed that resurrection of the dead referred to the resuscitation of corpses. Paul explains that resurrection entails transformation of the body into a new and glorious state.

Paul first uses the image of a plant springing forth from a seed (verses 36–38). The seed sown in the ground first dies, then it grows into a mature plant. No one could predict the form of the plant from the appearance of the seed. God is the one who determines what sort of body to give it. With this analogy Paul is able to demonstrate both the radical transformation of the human body in its resurrected state and yet its organic continuity with the mortal body that preceded it. Since our glorified state is indeed an embodied existence, Paul demonstrates that there are many different kinds of bodies in God's creation (verses 39–41). Each has its own distinct form, from the variety of animal life to the diverse heavenly bodies in the sky. Since each of these bodies possess varying degrees of glory, we can more easily imagine a different kind of human body, a glorified body unlike the bodies we now know.

Resurrection involves transformation into a new kind of body suitable for its new form of existence (verses 42–44). The body in this present life is perishable and weak; the body of those resurrected from the dead will be imperishable and glorious. What is sown is a natural, physical body; what is raised is a supernatural, spiritual body. Paul uses the representational figures of Adam and Christ to contrast humanity in its natural life and in its spiritual life to come (verses 45–49). We inherit one kind of body and life from Adam, "the man of dust," followed by a renewed, transformed body from Christ, "the man of heaven." We await the day when Christ, manifested in his resurrected body, will come from heaven to raise us and transform us into his likeness. On that final day, "we will all be changed" (verses 51–52), both the dead and those still alive, and our perishable, mortal bodies will put on imperishability and immortality (verses 53–54).

Though the "how" of resurrection still remains a mystery (verse 51), we know that God's plan for the end is not to destroy our bodies and start again but to transform our bodies, not to reject his creation but to redeem it. God's ultimate victory over of death is already assured, so we can even today sing a taunting victory song over the fallen enemy: "Where, O death, is your victory? Where, O death, is your sting?" (verses 55, 57). Death's stinging power to evoke fear, depression, and despair is already defeated through our Lord Jesus Christ. The final consequence of Christ's victory over death is stated in the last verse: We can do the work of the Lord with confident faith, knowing that in him everything we do has ultimate meaning and purpose (verse 58). Nothing we do in Christ is ever "in vain." We may not see the harvest in our lifetime, but a harvest there will indeed be.

Reflection and discussion

• What words would I use to explain the resurrected body to an unbeliever?

• Which words of Paul are most comforting for me? In what way do they take away the sting of death?

• How does Paul's teaching about resurrection lead me to do what he urges in verse 58?

Prayer

Thanks be to God who gives us the victory through our Lord Jesus Christ. You have destroyed the powers of death and given us hope and confidence in the future. Help me live a life that is worth living for eternity.

We know that if the earthly tent we live in is destroyed, we have a building from God, a house not made with hands, eternal in the heavens.

2 Cor 5:1

Clothed With Our Heavenly Dwelling

2 CORINTHIANS 4:7—5:10 *7But we have this treasure in clay jars, so that it may be made clear that this extraordinary power belongs to God and does not come from us. 8We are afflicted in every way, but not crushed; perplexed, but not driven to despair; 9persecuted, but not forsaken; struck down, but not destroyed; 10always carrying in the body the death of Jesus, so that the life of Jesus may also be made visible in our bodies. 11For while we live, we are always being given up to death for Jesus' sake, so that the life of Jesus may be made visible in our mortal flesh. 12So death is at work in us, but life in you.*

13But just as we have the same spirit of faith that is in accordance with scripture—"I believed, and so I spoke"—we also believe, and so we speak, 14because we know that the one who raised the Lord Jesus will raise us also with Jesus, and will bring us with you into his presence. 15Yes, everything is for your sake, so that grace, as it extends to more and more people, may increase thanksgiving, to the glory of God.

16So we do not lose heart. Even though our outer nature is wasting away, our inner nature is being renewed day by day. 17For this slight momentary affliction is preparing us for an eternal weight of glory beyond all measure, 18because we look not at what can be seen but at what cannot be seen; for what can be seen is temporary, but what cannot be seen is eternal.

5 *¹For we know that if the earthly tent we live in is destroyed, we have a building from God, a house not made with hands, eternal in the heavens. ²For in this tent we groan, longing to be clothed with our heavenly dwelling— ³if indeed, when we have taken it off we will not be found naked. ⁴For while we are still in this tent, we groan under our burden, because we wish not to be unclothed but to be further clothed, so that what is mortal may be swallowed up by life. ⁵He who has prepared us for this very thing is God, who has given us the Spirit as a guarantee. ⁶So we are always confident; even though we know that while we are at home in the body we are away from the Lord— ⁷for we walk by faith, not by sight. ⁸Yes, we do have confidence, and we would rather be away from the body and at home with the Lord. ⁹So whether we are at home or away, we make it our aim to please him. ¹⁰For all of us must appear before the judgment seat of Christ, so that each may receive recompense for what has been done in the body, whether good or evil.*

The heart of Paul's preaching and of all Christian believing is this statement: "We know that the one who raised the Lord Jesus will raise us also with Jesus" (4:14). Paul explains that this belief affects not only our future, but also our present. The resurrection of Jesus is the foundation for our hope; it is also the power presently at work within our mortal flesh. The gospel of Christ's resurrection is the treasure we possess in the "clay jars" of our bodies (4:7). In ordinary, fragile, earthen vessels dwells the "extraordinary power" to transform our bodies and make them like the risen body of Christ. In the first half of this passage Paul highlights the difference that the resurrection of Christ makes for the present (4:7–18); in the second half, the difference for the future (5:1–10).

Paul draws out the practical implications of the power of Christ's resurrection working within him through offering four vivid contrasts (4:8–9). He ought to be crushed, driven to despair, forsaken, and destroyed because of what he has been through. In fulfilling his call to be a minister of the gospel, Paul had known all kinds of trials (see 2 Cor 11:23–28). Understanding his own earthly life as a sharing in the crucified and risen Christ, Paul views all of these difficulties as "carrying in the body the death of Jesus" (4:10) and "being given up to death for Jesus' sake" (4:11). Yet simultaneously, he knows that the risen life of Jesus is made visible in his own body, even in his "mortal flesh." He experiences an indestructible power that is not his own always bearing him up and suffusing his present existence with visible signs of resurrection.

Paul presents his own life as an example for ours, "so we do not lose heart" (4:16). There is no escape from increasing physical weakness and suffering. Yet, "though our outer nature is wasting away, our inner nature is being renewed day by day." A process of destruction and reconstruction is constantly at work in us. We are being renewed and transformed through God's power already, though our inner nature will be perfected and completed in the resurrection of the dead. The afflictions that we experience are short-lived in comparison to the glory that awaits us (4:17). We are not able to see the goal God has in mind for us, but we live by faith and set our sights on what is eternal.

Paul uses three sets of images to symbolize the difference between life in this present world and the future life in the world to come. The first images contrast the present life as dwelling in tents and the future life in an eternal home (5:1). The transience and insecurity of this life's temporary dwelling is compared to the permanence and total security of dwelling with God. The second images express the passing from this life to the next as putting off and putting on clothes (5:2–4). At the end of earthly life, we will not be found naked, because God has prepared for us a new garment for eternal life. The final images contrast being away from the Lord and our final homecoming (5:6–9). The present life is only a partial fellowship with Christ—"we walk by faith, not by sight" (5:7)—but at the end of our final journey, we will be completely at home with the Lord.

Reflection and discussion

• What is the treasure we possess in clay jars? Why does Paul describe our lives as fragile, earthen vessels?

• What does Paul mean by "carrying in the body the death of Jesus"? How is the life of Jesus made visible in our bodies (4:10)?

• How can Paul's beliefs and experiences help me cope with my present troubles?

• Why does Paul use images to describe our future risen life? Which image is most helpful for my understanding?

Prayer

Faithful God, I know that you will raise me to eternal life just as you raised Jesus. You have prepared a secure home where I will live with you forever. Help me experience the power of resurrection in the fragile vessel of this life and hope in your promises for the future.

If we have been united with him in a death like his, we will certainly be united with him in a resurrection like his. Rom 6:5

Living in Newness of Life

ROMANS 6:3–14 *³Do you not know that all of us who have been baptized into Christ Jesus were baptized into his death? ⁴Therefore we have been buried with him by baptism into death, so that, just as Christ was raised from the dead by the glory of the Father, so we too might walk in newness of life.*

⁵For if we have been united with him in a death like his, we will certainly be united with him in a resurrection like his. ⁶We know that our old self was crucified with him so that the body of sin might be destroyed, and we might no longer be enslaved to sin. ⁷For whoever has died is freed from sin. ⁸But if we have died with Christ, we believe that we will also live with him. ⁹We know that Christ, being raised from the dead, will never die again; death no longer has dominion over him. ¹⁰The death he died, he died to sin, once for all; but the life he lives, he lives to God. ¹¹So you also must consider yourselves dead to sin and alive to God in Christ Jesus.

¹²Therefore, do not let sin exercise dominion in your mortal bodies, to make you obey their passions. ¹³No longer present your members to sin as instruments of wickedness, but present yourselves to God as those who have been brought from death to life, and present your members to God as instruments of righteousness. ¹⁴For sin will have no dominion over you, since you are not under law but under grace.

God acts in Christian baptism to join us to his Son. The effect of baptism is a profound identification with Christ, so that what is true of Christ becomes true of those who are baptized. When a person is "baptized into Christ Jesus" a very real change occurs. The believer's being is transformed and intimately united with Christ and his destiny.

The baptism of new Christians takes place at the Easter vigil in which the church celebrates the central mysteries of our faith. The convert descends into the baptismal pool, is covered with its waters, and emerges into a new life. The baptisteries of churches through the ages have been metaphorically compared to a tomb and a womb, because through baptism the believer dies with Christ and is born anew. The Christian Rite of Initiation culminates in the celebration of Eucharist in which the newly baptized receive the risen Christ, the bread of eternal life, in communion.

The death that the believer undergoes in baptism is a real dying with Christ. Paul refers to it as "baptized into his death" (verse 3). It even includes entering Christ's tomb: "buried with him by baptism into death" (verse 4). Since by dying on the cross Christ defeated sin, in our dying with Christ the power of sin no longer controls our lives. "Our old self was crucified" with Christ; therefore the dominating influence of sin has been destroyed and we are no longer enslaved to it (verse 6).

But that is only half of our baptism. In dying Christ conquered sin; in rising he conquered death. As Christ was raised from the dead, we too have the vitality of eternal life within us, so "we too might walk in newness of life" (verse 4). While Paul describes our dying with Christ with verbs in the past tense, he describes our rising with Christ in the future tense: "We will certainly be united with him in a resurrection like his" (verses 5, 8). The new life we have now is a prelude to our future resurrection. While we are truly "in Christ" by baptism, our lives are a step-by-step movement into Christ-likeness.

Our life in Christ today is an existence with one foot in the old life and one in the new. We live in the tension between sin and grace, flesh and spirit, death and life. Our fallen human nature pulls in one direction while our reborn life in Christ pulls even more powerfully in the other. We are already living in the risen Christ, and our freedom from sin and death is evident in the orientation of our lives. Yet the full realization of our resurrection awaits the future, when the full significance of Christ's dying and rising and of our baptism into him will become fully manifest.

Reflection and discussion

• Do I believe Paul's final statement: "Sin will have no dominion over you"? How do I struggle with the powers of sin?

• Do I look upon my baptism as a past event or a present reality? How do I try to renew and stir up the grace of my baptism?

• What aspect of my baptism have I overlooked or neglected? What is Paul teaching me anew in this passage?

Prayer

Crucified and Risen Lord, in baptism my old self was crucified and buried with you in the tomb. Renew the grace of baptism within me so that sin has no power in my life and I may walk in newness of life.

The creation itself will be set free from its bondage to decay and will obtain the freedom of the glory of the children of God. Rom 8:21

Waiting for the Redemption of Our Bodies

ROMANS 8:9–30 ⁹*But you are not in the flesh; you are in the Spirit, since the Spirit of God dwells in you. Anyone who does not have the Spirit of Christ does not belong to him. ¹⁰But if Christ is in you, though the body is dead because of sin, the Spirit is life because of righteousness. ¹¹If the Spirit of him who raised Jesus from the dead dwells in you, he who raised Christ from the dead will give life to your mortal bodies also through his Spirit that dwells in you.*

¹²*So then, brothers and sisters, we are debtors, not to the flesh, to live according to the flesh—¹³for if you live according to the flesh, you will die; but if by the Spirit you put to death the deeds of the body, you will live. ¹⁴For all who are led by the Spirit of God are children of God. ¹⁵For you did not receive a spirit of slavery to fall back into fear, but you have received a spirit of adoption. When we cry, "Abba! Father!" ¹⁶it is that very Spirit bearing witness with our spirit that we are children of God, ¹⁷and if children, then heirs, heirs of God and joint heirs with Christ—if, in fact, we suffer with him so that we may also be glorified with him.*

¹⁸*I consider that the sufferings of this present time are not worth comparing with the glory about to be revealed to us. ¹⁹For the creation waits with eager longing for the revealing of the children of God; ²⁰for the creation was sub-*

jected to futility, not of its own will but by the will of the one who subjected it, in hope [21]*that the creation itself will be set free from its bondage to decay and will obtain the freedom of the glory of the children of God.* [22]*We know that the whole creation has been groaning in labor pains until now;* [23]*and not only the creation, but we ourselves, who have the first fruits of the Spirit, groan inwardly while we wait for adoption, the redemption of our bodies.* [24]*For in hope we were saved. Now hope that is seen is not hope. For who hopes for what is seen?* [25]*But if we hope for what we do not see, we wait for it with patience.*

[26]*Likewise the Spirit helps us in our weakness; for we do not know how to pray as we ought, but that very Spirit intercedes with sighs too deep for words.* [27]*And God, who searches the heart, knows what is the mind of the Spirit, because the Spirit intercedes for the saints according to the will of God.*

[28]*We know that all things work together for good for those who love God, who are called according to his purpose.* [29]*For those whom he foreknew he also predestined to be conformed to the image of his Son, in order that he might be the firstborn within a large family.* [30]*And those whom he predestined he also called; and those whom he called he also justified; and those whom he justified he also glorified.*

Paul contrasts life in the flesh, that aspect of the human person that is closed and hostile to God, with life in the Spirit, that aspect that is open and responsive to God. Life in the flesh is under the dominion of sin and bound for death; life in the Spirit is lived in God's grace and bound for life eternal (verses 12–13). The ultimate source of the believer's vivifying power is the Holy Spirit, described by Paul in various ways: "the Spirit of God," "the Spirit of Christ" (verse 9), and "the Spirit of him who raised Jesus from the dead" (verse 11).

God sends his Spirit into the hearts of believers, reassuring them of God's irrevocable love for them and freeing them for praise, witness, and service. The Spirit integrates the objective achievement of Christ's dying and rising into the internal life of the person of faith. Ultimately, it is through this Spirit that God will give eternal life to our mortal bodies, but even now God's Spirit takes up residence within us (verse 11). Through this Spirit the saving work of Jesus is present for us and at work in us, offering us a foretaste of the life we will have in full at the final re-creation when our total being will be gloriously transformed.

Not only does the Holy Spirit live within us to orient our lives toward God and eternal life, the Spirit also makes us members of God's family. Through the Spirit of Christ within us, we are adopted by God and can address God in the same way Jesus did (verses 14–15). Sin makes us fearful slaves; God makes us trusting, confident children. With his Spirit within us, we share in all the privileges of Christ and become co-heirs with him of all the glory the Father has given to his Son (verses 16–17).

All of creation along with humanity awaits the future glory that God will give. While humanity suffers under the powers of sin and death, the material world is "subjected to futility" (verse 20) and under "bondage to decay" (verse 21). Both humanity and the whole creation have been "groaning in labor pains," awaiting redemption (verses 22–23). The suffering we experience in this life is painfully real, yet our suffering is dwarfed by the grandeur of glory to come (verse 18). The human and the nonhuman world long for wholeness and integrity, and the entire creation will be the arena for God's final redemptive work. Paul's vision of resurrection is cosmic, just as Isaiah had spoken of God renewing creation by fashioning "new heavens and a new earth" (Isa 65:17). Violated nature itself will be transformed and freed from decay and corruption.

The struggles that creation experiences now are labor pains, groaning and yearning for the time of deliverance. The hope that we share is more that a form of wishful thinking. It is a sure hope because we already have a down payment on its fulfillment. The Holy Spirit is the "firstfruits" (verse 23), that initial offering of the field that serves as a promise of the remainder of the harvest to come. God's Spirit is the ground of our hope for living in the tension between suffering and glory. It is this Holy Spirit that helps us in weakness and intercedes for us in prayer (verses 26–27). We have confidence in our future, finally, because we know it is in the hands of our all-powerful and loving God, not ours: "We know that all things work together for good for those who love God, who are called according to his purpose" (verse 28). Our destiny is firmly set in God's purposes: to transform us to the glorified image of Christ and to bring us into the family of God forever (verse 29–30).

Reflection and discussion

• What do verses 9 through 17 tell me about my relationship with God the Father, Son, and Holy Spirit?

• How aware am I of the presence of the Holy Spirit in my life? How could I live more fully a life in the Spirit?

• What distinguishes hope from wishful thinking? What makes our hope confident and certain?

Prayer

Come, Holy Spirit, you intercede for me, helping me to pray with sighs too deep for words. Give me a foretaste of the resurrection by bringing into my life the power of Christ's conquest of sin and death.

SUGGESTIONS FOR FACILITATORS, GROUP SESSION 3

1. Welcome group members and ask if there are any announcements anyone would like to make.

2. You may want to pray this prayer as a group:

Lord Jesus, through the writings of your apostle Paul, we learn the central importance of your resurrection for our Christian faith. Through the Holy Spirit, your resurrection is made visible in our own bodies, giving us confidence and assuring us that our earthly lives have meaning and purpose. Renew the grace of baptism in each of us and transform us through the power of your resurrection, so that we will experience the vitality of your life within us.

3. Ask one or more of the following questions:
   • What new insight into the meaning of resurrection did you gain this week?
   • What encouragement do you need to continue on the path of Bible reading?

4. Discuss lessons 7 through 12. Choose one or more of the questions for reflection and discussion from each lesson to talk over as a group. You may want to ask group members which question was most challenging or helpful to them as you review each lesson.

5. Keep the discussion moving, but don't rush it in order to complete more questions. Allow time for the questions that provoke the most discussion.

6. After talking about each lesson, instruct group members to complete lessons 13 through 18 on their own during the six days before the next group meeting. They should write out their own answers to the questions as preparation for next week's discussion.

7. Ask the group if anyone is having any particular problems with his or her Bible study during the week. You may want to share advice and encouragement within the group.

8. Conclude by praying aloud together the prayer at the end of one of the lessons discussed. You may add to the prayer based on the sharing that has occurred in the group.

He took her by the hand and said to her, "Talitha cum," which means,
"Little girl, get up!" And immediately the girl got up and began to walk about.

Mark 5:41–42

Jesus Restores a Little Girl to Life

MARK 5:21–23, 35–43 ²¹*When Jesus had crossed again in the boat to the other side, a great crowd gathered around him; and he was by the sea.* ²²*Then one of the leaders of the synagogue named Jairus came and, when he saw him, fell at his feet* ²³*and begged him repeatedly, "My little daughter is at the point of death. Come and lay your hands on her, so that she may be made well, and live."*

³⁵*While he was still speaking, some people came from the leader's house to say, "Your daughter is dead. Why trouble the teacher any further?"* ³⁶*But overhearing what they said, Jesus said to the leader of the synagogue, "Do not fear, only believe."* ³⁷*He allowed no one to follow him except Peter, James, and John, the brother of James.* ³⁸*When they came to the house of the leader of the synagogue, he saw a commotion, people weeping and wailing loudly.* ³⁹*When he had entered, he said to them, "Why do you make a commotion and weep? The child is not dead but sleeping."* ⁴⁰*And they laughed at him. Then he put them all outside, and took the child's father and mother and those who were with him, and went in where the child was.* ⁴¹*He took her by the hand and said to her, "Talitha cum," which means, "Little girl, get up!"* ⁴²*And immediately the girl got up and*

began to walk about (she was twelve years of age). At this they were overcome with amazement. ⁴³*He strictly ordered them that no one should know this, and told them to give her something to eat.*

The proclamation of Jesus' resurrection and narratives of his risen appearances come at the end of each of the four gospels. Yet the light of his resurrection illumines the entire gospel narrative and shines into each account of Jesus' life. This is particularly true in this narrative of Jesus raising the daughter of Jairus, the synagogue official.

In Mark's gospel the raising is set within the context of three other miracles, each demonstrating the power of Jesus. The calming of the storm (4:35–41) shows the power of Jesus over chaotic nature, the healing of the Gerasene demoniac (5:1–20) illustrates his authority over destructive demons, the healing of the woman with a hemorrhage (5:25–34) demonstrates his authority over debilitating illness, and finally this miracle proves Christ's lordship over even death itself.

Jairus fell at the feet of Jesus and earnestly beseeched Jesus to lay his hands on his little daughter so that she would be healed and live. The girl was "at the point of death" and the father is requesting that Jesus save her from the power of death. The terms used to describe Jairus's hope, that she may "be made well and live," also translate as "be saved and have life" (verse 23). These were terms used in early Christian circles for salvation and resurrected life, suggesting that Mark and the members of his Christian community saw the restoration to life of Jairus' daughter as an anticipation of the resurrected life of Jesus and of those who believe in him.

The next word from the messengers, "Your daughter is dead" (verse 35), heightens the drama and creates a seemingly hopeless situation. But the words of Jesus to Jairus, "Do not fear, only believe" (verse 36), link the effectiveness of Jesus' power to the faith of the girl's father. It is never too late to place trust in Jesus and hope in his power to give life. The weeping and loud wailing (verse 38) express the grief that death brings and the accompanying mourning rituals. The words of Jesus, "The child is not dead but sleeping" (verse 39), express the fact that all is not lost and that this dead child can be awakened again to life, perhaps hinting at Daniel 12:2 where the prophet proclaims that many of those who "sleep" shall "awake."

Jesus' raising the dead girl back to life is presented with both tender affection and sovereign authority (verses 41–42). The command of Jesus to "get up/arise" and the report that the girl "got up/arose" use two Greek verbs frequently used in the New Testament to express resurrection from the dead and Jesus' own resurrection. Jesus did not give the girl a true resurrection, that is, a transformed body that will never again die. Rather, he gave life back to her mortal corpse, and she would indeed die again in the future. Yet, this demonstration of Christ's power was, for the readers of Mark's gospel, a foreshadowing of the resurrection of Jesus and of our own final awakening from the sleep of death.

Reflection and discussion

• Describe how Jairus might have felt before and after his daughter's restoration to life?

• How does the context of this miracle add to my understanding of the power of Jesus?

• How does the light of Christ's resurrection illumine this account of Jairus and his daughter?

• In what way is the raising of the little girl a prefiguration of the resurrection, but not a true resurrection?

• Jesus told Jairus, "Do not fear, only believe." What is the relationship between crisis, fear, and faith in my life?

Prayer

Lord of power and might, you have authority over chaos, evil, sickness, and death. Be near me when death looms and relieve my fears. Give me the ability to trust in you and to know that "all things work together for good for those who love God" (Rom 8:28).

As they were coming down the mountain, he ordered them to tell no one about what they had seen, until after the Son of Man had risen from the dead. So they kept the matter to themselves, questioning what this rising from the dead could mean. Mark 9:9–10

He Will Rise From the Dead

MARK 9:2–10, 30–32 *²Six days later, Jesus took with him Peter and James and John, and led them up a high mountain apart, by themselves. And he was transfigured before them, ³and his clothes became dazzling white, such as no one on earth could bleach them. ⁴And there appeared to them Elijah with Moses, who were talking with Jesus. ⁵Then Peter said to Jesus, "Rabbi, it is good for us to be here; let us make three dwellings, one for you, one for Moses, and one for Elijah." ⁶He did not know what to say, for they were terrified. ⁷Then a cloud overshadowed them, and from the cloud there came a voice, "This is my Son, the Beloved; listen to him!" ⁸Suddenly when they looked around, they saw no one with them any more, but only Jesus.*

⁹As they were coming down the mountain, he ordered them to tell no one about what they had seen, until after the Son of Man had risen from the dead. ¹⁰So they kept the matter to themselves, questioning what this rising from the dead could mean.

³⁰They went on from there and passed through Galilee. He did not want any-one to know it; ³¹for he was teaching his disciples, saying to them, "The Son of

Man is to be betrayed into human hands, and they will kill him, and three days after being killed, he will rise again." [32] *But they did not understand what he was saying and were afraid to ask him.*

T he transfiguration of Jesus on the mountain was an experience reserved for the three closest disciples of Jesus, the same disciples who were called by Jesus to witness the raising of Jairus's daughter. Like the women at the empty tomb of Jesus, the disciples were "terrified" by the experience, an expression that denotes an awestruck amazement (verse 6; 16:8). They were commanded to silence about what they had seen until after the resurrection of Jesus (verse 9). This command to silence occurs frequently in Mark's gospel to express to the readers that it is impossible for anyone to truly understand Jesus until after the full manifestation of his mission in his death and resurrection. So they did not speak about their experience to others, but they continued to question "what rising from the dead could mean" (verse 10).

The confusion of the disciples over the meaning of resurrection is curious, since resurrection of the dead was a prominent belief among most of the Jews at the time. They trusted that the dead would be raised to life at the end of time. Their puzzlement must have been over how Jesus as an individual could be raised, since resurrection was understood as a collective event associated with the final day of the Lord. The transfiguration of Jesus offered them an anticipation of Christ's risen glory and a glimpse into its meaning in the context of God's saving plan.

Moses and Elijah, who appear with Jesus in glory, represent the law and the prophets of old and point to Jesus as the fulfillment of God's promises. The dazzling raiment of the transfigured Christ suggests a divine manifestation, like the visions of Old Testament prophets (verse 3). The cloud, a symbol of life and hope in a culture that depended on the regular cycle of rain, was likewise a manifestation of God's presence (verse 7). The language communicates in visual terms a fleeting and elusive perception of Christ's glorious splendor.

Though the transfiguration of Jesus prefigured his resurrection, the disciples and Mark's readers must recognize their call to an earthly mission of walking in the way of Jesus. The disciples continued to travel with Jesus, not yet comprehending that Jesus had to be betrayed and killed before his resurrection from the dead (verses 30–32). Only in the light of the resurrection would they begin to comprehend what they had experienced and understand their own role in God's saving plan.

Reflection and discussion

• Why did Jesus order his disciples not to tell anyone about what they had seen until after the resurrection?

• Why were the disciples puzzled over "what this rising from the dead could mean" (verse 10)?

• What experience in my life has helped me to gain a momentary glimpse of Christ's glory?

Prayer

Eternal Lord, you manifested your divine glory to your chosen disciples on the mountaintop. As I walk with you along the journey of life, give me glimpses of your divine splendor and instill within me a vibrant hope of the eternal glory you have promised.

When they rise from the dead, they neither marry nor are given in marriage, but are like angels in heaven. Mark 12:25

The Sadducees Question Jesus About the Resurrection

MARK 12:18–27 ¹⁸*Some Sadducees, who say there is no resurrection, came to him and asked him a question, saying,* ¹⁹*"Teacher, Moses wrote for us that 'if a man's brother dies, leaving a wife but no child, the man shall marry the widow and raise up children for his brother.'* ²⁰*There were seven brothers; the first married and, when he died, left no children;* ²¹*and the second married the widow and died, leaving no children; and the third likewise;* ²²*none of the seven left children. Last of all the woman herself died.* ²³*In the resurrection whose wife will she be? For the seven had married her."*

²⁴*Jesus said to them, "Is not this the reason you are wrong, that you know neither the scriptures nor the power of God?* ²⁵*For when they rise from the dead, they neither marry nor are given in marriage, but are like angels in heaven.* ²⁶*And as for the dead being raised, have you not read in the book of Moses, in the story about the bush, how God said to him, 'I am the God of Abraham, the God of Isaac, and the God of Jacob'?* ²⁷*He is God not of the dead, but of the living; you are quite wrong."*

The Sadducees were a movement within Judaism whose position on religious and political issues of the day often contrasted sharply with that of the Pharisees. This passage illustrates the two most distinctive positions of the Sadducees: there is no resurrection (verse 18; Acts 23:8) and there is no revelation apart from the Torah (the first five books of the Hebrew Bible). The question they ask of Jesus is not asked out of curiosity; it is intended to show that Jesus' teaching on resurrection is foolish.

The extreme case concocted by the Sadducees is based on the institution of levirate marriage in which a man has the right and duty to take his deceased brother's widow as his own wife and to have children with her (Deut 25:5–6). The illustration of the seven husbands being married to the same woman after resurrection is intended to reduce belief in resurrection to absurdity, evoking a bizarre image of an overcrowded bedroom.

The answer of Jesus is the twice affirmed, "You are wrong" (verses 24, 27). But as is typical of Jesus' argumentation, he turns the question back on his challengers to make them, and us, dig deeper. The case posed by the Sadducees assumes that resurrected life is very much like our present life, in which the norm is marriage between husband and wife and the begetting of children. But those who teach the resurrection of the dead (including Jesus and the Pharisees) envision a transformation to a new kind of existence. Jesus' instruction, that the resurrected existence will be "like angels in heaven" (verse 25), does not mean that the risen ones will be spirits without some sort of body, but that in their resurrected bodies they will be immortal and not identified by earthly relationships like marriage and begetting children. The resurrection does not simply mean resuscitation, like Jairus's daughter; rather the risen body is a totally transformed reality in which death has no more power.

Since the Sadducees only accepted revelation given in the Torah, and not in the other Old Testament passages that mention resurrection of the dead, Jesus offered a passage spoken three times by God to Moses at the burning bush: "I am the God of Abraham, the God of Isaac, and the God of Jacob" (verse 26; Exod 3:6, 15–16). These words were spoken by God as an assurance that he had remembered his covenant with the patriarchs and had come to deliver his people and bring them to freedom. Since God had promised Israel's patriarchs that he would be their savior and provider, his promise is meaningless if Abraham, Isaac, and Jacob have ceased to exist and are unable to enjoy his favor. Rather, the long–deceased patriarchs must have been in some sense still alive when God revealed himself to Moses and must still await the resurrection in the age to come.

The God who entered in covenant with the patriarchs and brought his people to freedom is "God not of the dead, but of the living" (verse 27). In Jesus, the God of the living is at work in a new way, a new exodus, in order to be the savior of his people. God's fidelity to the patriarchs would continue to operate; what God had done for Israel at the exodus would be fulfilled for the whole world in the resurrection from the dead.

Reflection and discussion

• What did the Sadducees intend to show by the case of the seven brothers? What is the flaw in their argument?

• Does Jesus' teaching about the resurrected state, "they neither marry nor are given in marriage," mean that I won't love my spouse in heaven or that I will love my spouse in a transformed and transcendent way? What makes me assume this is so?

Prayer

God of the covenant, your promises are eternal. Your desire to bring your people blessings, freedom, and life is renewed in every age. Let me trust in your promises that you will bring me from death to eternal life with you.

Very early on the first day of the week, when the sun had risen, they went to the tomb. Mark 16:2

The Tomb Where They Laid Him Is Empty

MARK 16:1–8 ¹*When the sabbath was over, Mary Magdalene, and Mary the mother of James, and Salome bought spices, so that they might go and anoint him.* ²*And very early on the first day of the week, when the sun had risen, they went to the tomb.* ³*They had been saying to one another, "Who will roll away the stone for us from the entrance to the tomb?"* ⁴*When they looked up, they saw that the stone, which was very large, had already been rolled back.* ⁵*As they entered the tomb, they saw a young man, dressed in a white robe, sitting on the right side; and they were alarmed.* ⁶*But he said to them, "Do not be alarmed; you are looking for Jesus of Nazareth, who was crucified. He has been raised; he is not here. Look, there is the place they laid him.* ⁷*But go, tell his disciples and Peter that he is going ahead of you to Galilee; there you will see him, just as he told you."* ⁸*So they went out and fled from the tomb, for terror and amazement had seized them; and they said nothing to anyone, for they were afraid.*

The announcement of Christ's resurrection is the climactic ending of Mark's Gospel. The narrative describes the women's discovery of the empty tomb on Sunday morning, "very early on the first day of the week, when the sun had risen" (verse 2). The Sabbath, the last day of the week, had ended (verse 1) and a new week was beginning. Genesis tells us that it was on the first day of the week that God began his creation. Mark describes the resurrection as the beginning of God's new creation. The "first day of the week" very quickly became the day when Christians met for worship (Acts 20:7). Soon the first day was known as "the Lord's day" (Rev 1:10). On this day, the church celebrates God's mighty act of raising Jesus from the dead. In this sense every Sunday is an Easter day. As the risen Lord, Christ has a claim on what we do with the first day of the week, as well as how we live and work from Monday to Saturday.

None of the Gospels give us an actual account of the resurrection. Rather, they relate what happened after the resurrection: the discovery of the empty tomb and the appearances of the risen Jesus. Clearly and concisely, Mark relates the fact of the empty tomb and the reason for its emptiness. The huge stone rolled away from the entrance to the tomb gives the first hint that the tomb is empty (verses 3–4). The young man dressed in white is the interpreting angel. The encounter is described in the familiar pattern of angelic messages: the angel appears, the receivers are fearful, the angel tells them not to fear and gives the explanation, the hearers receive a commission. The messenger's explanation for the empty tomb is startling: "He has been raised" (verse 6). The message brings a dramatic reversal to a tragic narrative that seemed to end in the abandonment and death of Christ. The messenger's commission to the women to go and tell the disciples that Jesus is going ahead of them to Galilee where they will see him (verse 7) offers a fresh beginning to the lives of those who has fled in denial and desertion. In that commission lies the promise of forgiveness and a renewed calling to follow him.

The end of Mark's gospel could be rightly called a cliffhanger. It ends quite abruptly: "they went out and fled from the tomb, for terror and amazement had seized them; and they said nothing to anyone, for they were afraid" (verse 8). The earliest gospel manuscripts end here, though there were several attempts by later editors to end the gospel in a more fitting manner. The so-called "shorter ending" and "longer ending" were clearly later additions to the gospel. Mark certainly knew the traditions of appearances of the risen Jesus and could have added them here. But Mark wanted to put the emphasis elsewhere. Writing to teach people in the generation after Jesus how to be disciples, Mark leaves his gospel open-ended. The resurrection is not the end of the story, but only a new beginning. The final message is that Jesus has gone ahead of his disciples. Mark leaves the gospel incomplete because the good news of Jesus is incomplete. The risen Christ continued to lead those who choose to follow him. It is up to each individual in every generation to come to know and experience the risen presence of Jesus.

The last thing the women expected to see was an empty tomb, and, rather than joy, the closing verses are expressions of fright and bewilderment: "they were alarmed"(verse 5), "terror and amazement had seized them (verse 8); and the final words of the gospel, "they were afraid." These are the emotions experienced by those who witnessed the raising of Jairus's daughter (5:42) and the transfiguration of Jesus (9:6), the natural response to a mighty act of God. The emotional response of the grieving women is understandable. Dead people don't rise—truly they do on the last day, but not in the here and now. Our difficulty is that we have heard the story so often that we fail to react because we know how it ends. But that is just Mark's point; we don't know how it will end. The gospel is incomplete and open-ended, to be completed with our own lives recreated by God in the light of the risen Christ. Christians must recover a sense of frightful amazement at the resurrection.

Reflection and discussion

• What is the significance in the fact that Christ rose on the first day of the week?

• What about this resurrection account reminds me that the Christ of Easter day is the Christ of every day?

• In what way is the response of the women natural and honest? What does their reaction teach me about my response to the risen Lord?

• Why does Mark's gospel not end with appearances of the risen Jesus like the other three gospels?

• What is Mark trying to communicate to me with the abrupt ending to his gospel?

Prayer

Glorious God, you raised Jesus with your mighty power and defeated the powers of sin and death. Instill within me a holy fear and tremendous awe at the wondrous act of resurrection.

They went with the guard and made the tomb secure by sealing the stone.
Matt 27:66

Rolling Back the Stone of the Empty Tomb

MATTHEW 27:62—28:10 ⁶²*The next day, that is, after the day of Preparation, the chief priests and the Pharisees gathered before Pilate* ⁶³*and said, "Sir, we remember what that impostor said while he was still alive, 'After three days I will rise again.' * ⁶⁴*Therefore command the tomb to be made secure until the third day; otherwise his disciples may go and steal him away, and tell the people, 'He has been raised from the dead,' and the last deception would be worse than the first." * ⁶⁵*Pilate said to them, "You have a guard of soldiers; go, make it as secure as you can." * ⁶⁶*So they went with the guard and made the tomb secure by sealing the stone.*

28 ¹*After the sabbath, as the first day of the week was dawning, Mary Magdalene and the other Mary went to see the tomb.* ²*And suddenly there was a great earthquake; for an angel of the Lord, descending from heaven, came and rolled back the stone and sat on it.* ³*His appearance was like lightning, and his clothing white as snow.* ⁴*For fear of him the guards shook and became like dead men.* ⁵*But the angel said to the women, "Do not be afraid; I know that you are looking for Jesus who was crucified.* ⁶*He is not here; for he has been raised, as he said. Come, see the place where he lay.* ⁷*Then go quickly and tell his disciples,*

'He has been raised from the dead, and indeed he is going ahead of you to Galilee; there you will see him.' This is my message for you." ⁸So they left the tomb quickly with fear and great joy, and ran to tell his disciples. ⁹Suddenly Jesus met them and said, "Greetings!" And they came to him, took hold of his feet, and worshiped him. ¹⁰Then Jesus said to them, "Do not be afraid; go and tell my brothers to go to Galilee; there they will see me."

The resurrection narrative in Matthew's gospel is significantly different from that of Mark's gospel. Matthew is the only gospel to interject the tradition that the tomb was placed under surveillance on the suspicion that the disciples would attempt to steal the body and fabricate a resurrection story. The account reflects the radically different explanations of the empty tomb between Jews and Christians in Matthew's time. The Jewish leaders explained the empty tomb as a hoax by charging that the disciples had stolen the body of Jesus. Christians proclaimed that the tomb was empty because of God's triumphant power in raising Jesus from the dead. Matthew assures his readers that Jesus' body has not been stolen since the Jewish leaders had sealed the tomb and set a guard over it.

The narrative ironically prepares the reader for the resurrection account. First, the Jewish leaders recall that Jesus had stated, "After three days I will rise again" (27:63). Indeed, Jesus had foretold his future death and resurrection three times in Matthew's gospel. Second, the leaders fear that his disciples will tell the people, "He has been raised from the dead" (27:64). To be sure, this good news did break forth and became the core of early Christian preaching. Finally, Pilate told the leaders to place their own soldier at the tomb and to "make it as secure as you can" (27:65). But in fact no matter how securely the tomb was guarded, they could not prevent the glorious resurrection.

Only Matthew mentions "a great earthquake" and the angel rolling back the stone from the tomb (28:2). The earthquake points to the world-changing and earth-shattering implications of Christ's resurrection. Its seismic repercussions continue to reverberate down through the course of history. Though its magnitude rocked the very foundations of the earth, its impact was not destructive, but life-creating and hope-inducing.

The angel's action of rolling back the stone and sitting upon it triumphantly expresses the fact that death has been routed. There is no indication that the angel rolled back the stone to let Jesus out of the tomb. Surely there are no barriers to the risen Lord. But the stone was rolled away for the sake of the women, so they could see that the tomb was empty.

The response of the women to the command of the angel is described as both "fear" and "joy" (28:8). Those who struggle to understand the simultaneous experience of these seemingly opposite sensations should consider the emotions of one about to be married. As the women were rushing to tell the apostles the news, the risen Jesus met them and greeted them. In response, the women prostrated themselves before him and clasped his feet (28:9). This is one of the many ways the gospel writers tell the reader that the risen Jesus was not a disembodied spirit, but a real, yet transformed person who could be grasped. Jesus did not allow the women to linger in adoration, but encouraged them to go fearlessly on their mission of proclaiming the good news.

Reflection and discussion

• What is the significance of the earthquake and the angel's rolling back the stone?

• When have I been both fearful and joyful? Is this a characteristic response to the action of God?

Prayer

Risen Lord, I fear the awesome power manifested at your resurrection and I rejoice in the good news of your rising. I want to grasp your feet and worship you, but you have sent me to bring the good news of resurrection to your people. Please urge me on my way.

The eleven disciples went to Galilee, to the mountain to which Jesus had directed them. When they saw him, they worshiped him; but some doubted.

Matt 28:16–17

The Appearance of Jesus to His Disciples in Galilee

MATTHEW 28:11–20 ¹¹*While they were going, some of the guard went into the city and told the chief priests everything that had happened.* ¹²*After the priests had assembled with the elders, they devised a plan to give a large sum of money to the soldiers,* ¹³*telling them, "You must say, 'His disciples came by night and stole him away while we were asleep.'* ¹⁴*If this comes to the governor's ears, we will satisfy him and keep you out of trouble."* ¹⁵*So they took the money and did as they were directed. And this story is still told among the Jews to this day.*

¹⁶*Now the eleven disciples went to Galilee, to the mountain to which Jesus had directed them.* ¹⁷*When they saw him, they worshiped him; but some doubted.* ¹⁸*And Jesus came and said to them, "All authority in heaven and on earth has been given to me.* ¹⁹*Go therefore and make disciples of all nations, baptizing them in the name of the Father and of the Son and of the Holy Spirit,* ²⁰*and teaching them to obey everything that I have commanded you. And remember, I am with you always, to the end of the age."*

The empty tomb is an external support for Christian faith, but by itself it does not prove the resurrection of Jesus. The emptiness of the tomb has been explained in several ways through the centuries: the women went to the wrong tomb, Jesus never really died, or the disciples stole the body of Jesus. Matthew shows how the latter story arose and why it should not be believed. Having failed to prevent the resurrection, the religious leaders tried to render it unbelievable. Of all the possible explanations for the empty tomb, Matthew proposes the announcement of the angel and the proclamation of the early church, "He has been raised," as the only true one.

"When they saw him" (verse 16) indicates that the risen Jesus appeared to the eleven disciples in Galilee. They worshipped him, but some doubted (verse 17). "Doubt" here implies weakness in faith or hesitation. This mixture of faith and uncertainty is characteristic of Christian discipleship until the close of the age. But because the authority and power of Jesus has been made universal by his resurrection (verse 18), Jesus commissions his disciples to a worldwide mission (verse 19). The mission of the disciples, previously restricted by Jesus, is now directed to all people, Jews and Gentiles. Jesus commands them to "go" to the nations. The people of the world will not come unless the disciples go to them.

The commissioning of the disciples reflects the threefold mission of the church: evangelization, baptism, and teaching. The initial task is the proclamation of the good news. Then new disciples are brought into the life of the church through baptism. Finally, detailed teaching in the way of Christ must guide the new disciples. But this entire mission of the disciples is possible only because of the final promise of the risen Lord: "I am with you always, to the end of the age" (verse 20). The abiding presence of Jesus is with his church, giving confidence to disciples in every age as they await his final coming in glory.

Reflection and discussion

• What explanations have been put forward for the empty tomb? How might they be refuted?

• If the empty tomb is not proof that Christ rose from the dead, what is the greatest verification of his resurrection?

• What is the three-fold mission given to the disciples of Jesus? In what ways am I carrying out Christ's great commission?

Prayer

Savior and Lord, you have risen from the tomb and brought hope to the world. Help me believe that you are with me always and give me the courage to carry out the mission you have given me as your disciple in the world today.

SUGGESTIONS FOR FACILITATORS, GROUP SESSION 4

1. Welcome group members and ask if anyone has any questions, announcements, or requests.

2. You may want to pray this prayer as a group:

Son of the Living God, the light of your resurrection illumines every part of the gospel accounts. Your teachings and healings all demonstrate that you want to save your people from fear and darkness and offer us life and salvation. As we read the gospels, deepen our amazement and joy at the wonders of your resurrection and increase our hope and determination as you send us out into the world. Help us realize that your gospel is always open-ended, and that we continue and complete the good news through our life in you.

3. Ask one or more of the following questions:
- What is the most difficult part of this study for you?
- What did you learn about the gospels this week?

4. Discuss lessons 13 through 18. Choose one or more of the questions for reflection and discussion from each lesson to discuss as a group. You may want to ask group members which question was most challenging or helpful to them as you review each lesson.

5. Keep the discussion moving, but allow time for the questions that provoke the most discussion. Encourage the group members to use "I" language in their responses.

6. After talking over each lesson, instruct group members to complete lessons 19 through 24 on their own during the six days before the next group meeting. They should write out their own answers to the questions as preparation for next week's session.

7. Conclude by praying aloud together the prayer at the end of one of the lessons discussed. You may choose to conclude the prayer by asking members to pray aloud any requests they may have.

It was Mary Magdalene, Joanna, Mary the mother of James,
and the other women with them who told this to the apostles. Luke 24:10

Why Look for the
Living Among the Dead?

LUKE 24:1–12 *¹But on the first day of the week, at early dawn, they came to the tomb, taking the spices that they had prepared. ²They found the stone rolled away from the tomb, ³but when they went in, they did not find the body. ⁴While they were perplexed about this, suddenly two men in dazzling clothes stood beside them. ⁵The women were terrified and bowed their faces to the ground, but the men said to them, "Why do you look for the living among the dead? He is not here, but has risen. ⁶Remember how he told you, while he was still in Galilee, ⁷that the Son of Man must be handed over to sinners, and be crucified, and on the third day rise again." ⁸Then they remembered his words, ⁹and returning from the tomb, they told all this to the eleven and to all the rest. ¹⁰Now it was Mary Magdalene, Joanna, Mary the mother of James, and the other women with them who told this to the apostles. ¹¹But these words seemed to them an idle tale, and they did not believe them. ¹²But Peter got up and ran to the tomb; stooping and looking in, he saw the linen cloths by themselves; then he went home, amazed at what had happened.*

E ach gospel writer has his own distinctive emphases in telling the resurrection narrative. For Luke, the visit to the empty tomb and the resurrection appearances of Jesus form the climax of his total plan for the gospel and form a transition to his second volume, the Acts of the Apostles. For this reason, Luke does not narrate any resurrection appearances in Galilee, but keeps Jerusalem as the focal point. This is the city of Jesus' destiny, the place where the risen Jesus meets his disciples, and the place from which the ministry of the early church goes forth. Luke follows the pattern of the Hebrew prophet: "For out of Zion shall go forth instruction, the word of the Lord from Jerusalem" (Micah 4:2). The movement of the Acts of the Apostles proceeds from Jerusalem "to the ends of the earth" (Acts 1:8).

The words of the angels to the women are unique to Luke's gospel. Perplexed about not finding the body of Jesus in the tomb, the women are asked by the two men in dazzling clothes, "Why do you look for the living among the dead?" (verse 5). This is similar to the question asked by the two men in white garments at the ascension of Jesus, "Why do you stand looking up toward heaven?" (Acts 1:11). In each case the question challenges the hearers to take up their new task, and each question is followed by a proclamation that sets them off on their mission.

There is no appearance of the risen Christ at the empty tomb in Luke's account. Instead, Luke builds up evidence for the bodily resurrection. The first hint is found in the women's discovery that the stone had been rolled away (verse 2). When the women entered the tomb, they found it empty; the body of Jesus was gone (verse 3). After the report of the women, Peter sets off for the tomb and repeats the discovery process of the women. Looking into the tomb, "he saw the linen cloths by themselves" (verse 12). This bit of evidence was significant, for if anyone wanted to remove the body of Jesus, they would not have left the grave clothes behind. They would have most likely carried the body away in its shroud. So the presence of the linen cloths is yet another indication of the bodily resurrection.

The stress on the empty tomb and the absence of Christ's body expresses the fact that the resurrection is something that happened to Jesus and is not just a subjective experience in the minds of his disciples. The disciples were changed because they discovered that the body of Jesus had been transformed through resurrection. The empty tomb witnesses that the body of Jesus was not there, distinguishing resurrection from the Greek teaching on the immortality of the soul. Jesus rose with a body that was recognizably his own, though transformed. The empty tomb also connects the resurrection with the crucifixion. The risen body was the body of the crucified. In raising Jesus, God put his seal of everlasting approval on the work of Jesus on the cross.

Reflection and discussion

• Why does Luke report only resurrection traditions that occurred in or around Jerusalem? In what way does his resurrection narrative tie together his two-volume work?

• How does the empty tomb add to the evidence for the objective and historical nature of the resurrection?

Prayer

Crucified and risen Lord, fill me with astonishment and awe at the mystery of your resurrection. Lead me as I discover, like your first disciples, the wonderful good news of your risen life.

While they were talking and discussing, Jesus himself came near and went with them, but their eyes were kept from recognizing him. Luke 24:15–16

Appearance on the Way to Emmaus

LUKE 24:13–27 ¹³*Now on that same day two of them were going to a village called Emmaus, about seven miles from Jerusalem, ¹⁴and talking with each other about all these things that had happened. ¹⁵While they were talking and discussing, Jesus himself came near and went with them, ¹⁶but their eyes were kept from recognizing him. ¹⁷And he said to them, "What are you discussing with each other while you walk along?" They stood still, looking sad. ¹⁸Then one of them, whose name was Cleopas, answered him, "Are you the only stranger in Jerusalem who does not know the things that have taken place there in these days?" ¹⁹He asked them, "What things?" They replied, "The things about Jesus of Nazareth, who was a prophet mighty in deed and word before God and all the people, ²⁰and how our chief priests and leaders handed him over to be condemned to death and crucified him. ²¹But we had hoped that he was the one to redeem Israel. Yes, and besides all this, it is now the third day since these things took place. ²²Moreover, some women of our group astounded us. They were at the tomb early this morning, ²³and when they did not find his body there, they came back and told us that they had indeed seen a vision of angels who said that he was alive. ²⁴Some of those who were with us went to the tomb and found it just as the women had said; but they did not see him." ²⁵Then he said to them,*

"Oh, how foolish you are, and how slow of heart to believe all that the prophets have declared! ²⁶*Was it not necessary that the Messiah should suffer these things and then enter into his glory?"* ²⁷*Then beginning with Moses and all the prophets, he interpreted to them the things about himself in all the scriptures.*

After the account of the visit to the empty tomb, each gospel writer goes his own way in the resurrection narrative. Luke recounts an appearance of the risen Jesus to two disciples traveling home from Jerusalem after the Passover feast. The "two of them" (verse 13) refers back to the previous scene, to the group of disciples who had been with the eleven to hear the report of the women after their return from the empty tomb (verses 9, 22–24). The fact that Cleophas is mentioned only here and the other traveler remains anonymous points to the fact that this appearance of Jesus could have occurred with any of Christ's followers, not just with the well-known apostles. The location of Emmaus has been much disputed and the note that the village is sixty stadia from Jerusalem, or about seven miles, has not helped biblical geographers determine its precise place. For Luke's purposes, it is only important that it be near Jerusalem, and the fact that Emmaus seems to be a village of indeterminate location seems to emphasize the fact that this appearance occurred with ordinary, small-town folk.

The walk to Emmaus took place "on that same day" (verse 13), that is, the first day of the week, the day of the resurrection. All of the resurrection events of Luke's gospel happen on this same day. This is the day of the week on which the early Christians would soon begin their weekly gathering for the Eucharist, most often in the evenings since the first day of the week was an ordinary workday in Jewish and Roman societies. We can assume that the two travelers were returning home from their pilgrimage to Jerusalem, during which they experienced the heart-breaking crucifixion of Jesus.

Not surprisingly, they were talking about everything that had happened (verse 14)—Jesus' torturous death, their disappointed hopes, and the women's report of the empty tomb. When Jesus came up to them, he must have seemed like another pilgrim returning home (verse 15). Cleopas' question, "Are you the only stranger in Jerusalem who does not know the things that have taken place there in these days?" (verse 18), assumes that the crucifixion of Jesus was the talk of Jerusalem during the Passover feast. But ironically it was not

Jesus who did not know, but rather Cleopas and his companion. The two disciples express their sadness at the death of Jesus (verse 17), their disappointment and shattered hopes (verse 21), and their skepticism at the women's report (verses 22–24).

The response of Jesus is surprisingly forceful, especially as he reproaches them for not taking the Scriptures seriously regarding the suffering and glorification of the Messiah (verses 25–26). As Peter would later explain, the crucifixion of Jesus was no tragic accident, but part of God's "definite plan and foreknowledge" (Acts 2:23). Jesus' interpretation of the Scriptures to them does not seem to refer to any particular passage. Rather, he laid out for them the way in which "all the scriptures" had led up to God's revelation of the cross and resurrection of Christ, "beginning with Moses and all the prophets" (verse 27). What a Bible study that must have been, as the risen Lord "interpreted" the Scriptures for them!

Reflection and discussion

• What does the obscurity of the two disciples and of their home town tell me about my relationship with Jesus?

• What was the probable tone and content of the disciples' conversation on their journey to Emmaus? In what ways does their exchange remind me of the way I often converse?

• In what way do the words of Jesus to his two disciples remind me of the necessity of knowing the Old Testament in order to understand him?

• Why does Jesus not immediately reveal himself to the two disciples?

• In what way do I depend on the risen Lord to interpret the Scriptures for me?

Prayer

Lord Jesus, you guide us through the Scriptures to understand God's plan and the significance of your life for us. Assure me of your presence with me when I study the Bible so that my heart will burn with love as I recognize your presence.

When he was at the table with them, he took bread, blessed and broke it, and gave it to them. Then their eyes were opened, and they recognized him.

Luke 24:30–31

Open Eyes in the Breaking of the Bread

LUKE 24:28–35 ²⁸*As they came near the village to which they were going, he walked ahead as if he were going on.* ²⁹*But they urged him strongly, saying, "Stay with us, because it is almost evening and the day is now nearly over." So he went in to stay with them.* ³⁰*When he was at the table with them, he took bread, blessed and broke it, and gave it to them.* ³¹*Then their eyes were opened, and they recognized him; and he vanished from their sight.* ³²*They said to each other, "Were not our hearts burning within us while he was talking to us on the road, while he was opening the scriptures to us?"* ³³*That same hour they got up and returned to Jerusalem; and they found the eleven and their companions gathered together.* ³⁴*They were saying, "The Lord has risen indeed, and he has appeared to Simon!"* ³⁵*Then they told what had happened on the road, and how he had been made known to them in the breaking of the bread.*

As evening descended, when the day of resurrection was nearly over, the two disciples convince Jesus to stay with them (verse 29). Reclining at the table at the time of the evening meal, the guest became the host. When Jesus "took bread, blessed and broke it, and gave it" to his disciples, they recognized him (verses 30–31). His gestures look back to the action of the Last Supper and ahead to the "breaking of the bread" in Acts.

As the narrative reaches its climax and Jesus then vanishes from their sight, the disciples realize that it was Christ's risen presence they were experiencing all along. They remembered that their hearts were burning with insight and love as Jesus interpreted the Scriptures for them (verse 32). Only after understanding the Scriptures were they prepared to recognize Jesus in the breaking of the bread.

The Emmaus account was written with Christian worship in mind. The disciples and Luke's readers now realize how the risen Lord will be present to his church. The account demonstrates the dynamic relationship between word and sacrament, and it reflects the twofold structure of the Christian assembly. Both the interpretation of the Scriptures and the breaking of the bread are actions of the risen Christ in which his presence is made real for the church.

But it is not only word and sacrament that suggests the Eucharist; it is also found in the movement from table to witnessing to others. The disciples returned at once to Jerusalem to communicate their experience of how they came to know the risen Christ (verses 33–35). The narrative began with the disciples walking slowly and hopelessly from Jerusalem to Emmaus; it ends with their movement hurriedly and expectantly from Emmaus to Jerusalem.

The Emmaus account describes, in narrative form, the process by which the first believers learned to recognize the significance of the events they witnessed. The resurrection shed new light on Jesus' death, on his words, and on the ancient Scriptures. When they first encountered Jesus, the disciples were blind to all the evidence that pointed to the risen Christ. At the beginning of the account, "their eyes were kept from recognizing him" (verse 16); toward the end of the narrative, "their eyes were opened, and they recognized him" (verse 31). As Jesus opened the text of Scripture for them, their hearts and minds and eyes began to open. Then open eyes, minds, and hearts led to open mouths. Once they had experienced Jesus alive, they could not keep the news to themselves. They joined their witness to that of Simon Peter and the believers in Jerusalem, communicating their experiences and becoming a worshiping and witnessing community of disciples.

Reflection and discussion

• What does the Emmaus account teach me about the ways that Jesus reveals himself to me today?

• What indicates that Luke wrote this account in the context of Christian worship? What does the narrative instruct the church about their celebration of the Eucharist?

• In what way does coming to understand the Scriptures open my eyes to know and recognize Jesus?

Prayer

Glorified Christ, open the Scriptures to me, so that you may also open my eyes, mind, and heart to you. Walk with me along the road of life and teach me to recognize your risen presence in the many ways you make yourself known.

Look at my hands and my feet; see that it is I myself. Touch me and see; for a ghost does not have flesh and bones as you see that I have.
Luke 24:39

The Risen Jesus Promises the Spirit's Power

LUKE 24:36–53 ³⁶*While they were talking about this, Jesus himself stood among them and said to them, "Peace be with you." ³⁷They were startled and terrified, and thought that they were seeing a ghost. ³⁸He said to them, "Why are you frightened, and why do doubts arise in your hearts? ³⁹Look at my hands and my feet; see that it is I myself. Touch me and see; for a ghost does not have flesh and bones as you see that I have." ⁴⁰And when he had said this, he showed them his hands and his feet. ⁴¹While in their joy they were disbelieving and still wondering, he said to them, "Have you anything here to eat?" ⁴²They gave him a piece of broiled fish, ⁴³and he took it and ate in their presence.*

⁴⁴*Then he said to them, "These are my words that I spoke to you while I was still with you—that everything written about me in the law of Moses, the prophets, and the psalms must be fulfilled." ⁴⁵Then he opened their minds to understand the scriptures, ⁴⁶and he said to them, "Thus it is written, that the Messiah is to suffer and to rise from the dead on the third day, ⁴⁷and that repentance and forgiveness of sins is to be proclaimed in his name to all nations, beginning from Jerusalem. ⁴⁸You are witnesses of these things. ⁴⁹And see, I am sending upon you*

what my Father promised; so stay here in the city until you have been clothed with power from on high."

⁵⁰Then he led them out as far as Bethany, and, lifting up his hands, he blessed them. ⁵¹While he was blessing them, he withdrew from them and was carried up into heaven. ⁵²And they worshiped him, and returned to Jerusalem with great joy; ⁵³and they were continually in the temple blessing God.

This final resurrection appearance of Luke's gospel parallels the Emmaus account in several ways. In both scenes Jesus' risen presence is not understood, but both culminate in an explanation of the importance of Scripture for understanding the person and ministry of Jesus. These two appearance narratives are also similar in that both times Jesus eats and both times the unbelief and incomprehension of the disciples give way to belief and understanding.

The risen reality of Jesus is impossible to completely describe or understand because it belongs to the age to come, rather than to the limitations of the present age. Each gospel writer struggles to express different aspects of the transcendent Christ in human words, knowing that his risen presence is ultimately indescribable. The emphasis in this account is on Jesus being bodily present. The disciples first thought they were seeing some kind of insubstantial, ghostly presence (verse 37). But Jesus emphasized his "flesh and bones" (verse 39), suggesting that he shares a common humanity with them. He invited them to look at his hands and feet, to touch him in order to know that his body is real. The narrative counters arguments that the disciples perhaps saw nothing more than a fleeting vision or a grief-induced hallucination. Jesus is indeed real and recognizable. He even eats a piece of broiled fish in their presence as a final proof, since ghosts and visions do not eat (verse 42–43). "See that it is I myself," Jesus insists. Surely this was the same Jesus who lived among them before his death. The risen Lord is the man of Galilee.

The appearance of Jesus elicits a number of emotional reactions from his disciples. At first they are startled, terrified, frightened, incredulous (verse 37–38). Yet, Jesus stands in the midst of them and says, "Peace be with you" (verse 36). His greeting of peace wishes for the receiver a fullness and wholeness that is brought by Christ's victory over all sources of fear. After Jesus demonstrated that he was real, their fear turned to joy, though they were still disbelieving (verse 41). But now their unbelief seems to have more to do with the feeling that it is all too good to be true.

Jesus opens his disciples' minds by opening the Scriptures to them. In light of the resurrection, it is possible to understand how the entire saving plan of God, made known in the law, the prophets, and the psalms, is fulfilled in the death and resurrection of Jesus (verses 44–46). Jesus commissions his disciples for the decisive role they are to play in the new phase of salvation history: they are to be witnesses to Christ, proclaiming repentance and forgiveness, beginning in Jerusalem and extending to all the nations (verses 47–48). It is this witness of the disciples that is the subject of Luke's Acts of the Apostles. The goal of Jesus' journey, Jerusalem, now becomes the starting point from which the message of salvation will extend to the ends of the earth (Acts 1:8).

The gospel ends with Christ's promise to send the Holy Spirit and his ascension into heaven. Though his bodily appearances have come to an end, his church will continue to experience his risen and glorified presence and activity in numerous ways. At the end of the gospel, the disciples are left waiting in Jerusalem. Luke's sequel volume will continue the story of Christ's church, beginning with the descent of God's Holy Spirit and the empowerment of the disciples as witnesses to all the nations.

Reflection and discussion

• In what ways does Luke try to convince his readers that Jesus' appearances were not just visions or hallucinations? What most convinces me?

• In what ways is the church a witness to Christ in the world today? How is my life a part of that witness?

• Why is it impossible to completely describe the risen presence of Jesus?

• Why does Jesus open the minds of his disciples to understand "the law of Moses, the prophets and the psalms"?

• In what ways does the church continue to experience the risen and glorified presence of Jesus today?

Prayer

Lord Jesus, send the power of your Holy Spirit upon me so that I may be a witness to the forgiveness you offer in your cross and resurrection. Continue to make yourself known to me in word, sacrament, and the lives of your people.

God raised him up, having freed him from death, because it was impossible for him to be held in its power. Acts 2:24

Peter Proclaims the Resurrection in Jerusalem

ACTS 2:22–32 ²²*"You that are Israelites, listen to what I have to say: Jesus of Nazareth, a man attested to you by God with deeds of power, wonders, and signs that God did through him among you, as you yourselves know—* ²³*this man, handed over to you according to the definite plan and foreknowledge of God, you crucified and killed by the hands of those outside the law.* ²⁴*But God raised him up, having freed him from death, because it was impossible for him to be held in its power.* ²⁵*For David says concerning him,*

'I saw the Lord always before me,
for he is at my right hand so that I will not be shaken;
²⁶*therefore my heart was glad, and my tongue rejoiced;*
moreover my flesh will live in hope.
²⁷*For you will not abandon my soul to Hades,*
or let your Holy One experience corruption.
²⁸*You have made known to me the ways of life;*
you will make me full of gladness with your presence.'

²⁹*'Fellow Israelites, I may say to you confidently of our ancestor David that he both died and was buried, and his tomb is with us to this day.* ³⁰*Since he was a*

prophet, he knew that God had sworn with an oath to him that he would put one of his descendants on his throne. [31]*Foreseeing this, David spoke of the resurrection of the Messiah, saying,*

'*He was not abandoned to Hades,*
  nor did his flesh experience corruption.'

[32]*This Jesus God raised up, and of that all of us are witnesses.*"

T he Acts of the Apostles is about the witness of the apostles. In its programmatic verse, the risen Jesus says, "You will receive power when the Holy Spirit has come upon you; and you will be my witnesses in Jerusalem, in all Judea and Samaria, and to the ends of the earth" (Acts 1:8). The first half of the book is largely concerned with the witness of Peter; the second half with the witness of Paul.

In Acts, much of the witness of the apostles takes the form of speeches. Almost a third of the book is taken up with these sermons, mostly by Peter and Paul. In all of these speeches the resurrection occupies the central place. The apostles preached the good news of Jesus risen from the dead. Jesus is Lord because God has raised him from the dead. As Peter proclaimed, "This Jesus God raised up, and of that all of us are witnesses" (verse 32).

After the Holy Spirit came with power upon the apostles, Peter addressed the crowd that had gathered in amazement. The focus of his sermon is Jesus of Nazareth. After a brief summary of his life and ministry, he directs his attention to the death of Jesus on the cross. Even in this terrible event, God was at work (verses 22–23). The cross was no unfortunate accident, but part of the divine plan foreshadowed in the ancient scriptures. But God raised Jesus up (verse 24), reversing his crucifixion and death imposed by human hands. God freed Jesus from the bondage of death that holds humanity in its grip.

Because the resurrection sheds new light on the scriptures of the Old Testament, Peter launches into an extended quotation from Psalm 16. In its original setting, the psalm is a hymn of praise to God, who saved the psalmist by protecting him from death. But Peter dramatically reinterprets the message of the psalm in the light of Christ, applying its words to the restoration of the body after the grave. Though King David is the traditional source of the psalms, Peter states that David clearly did not write this psalm about himself, for it speaks of one who is alive. David was buried in a tomb in Jerusalem (verse 29). The psalm is rather about David's descendant, whom God promised to put on David's throne as the Messiah. As a prophet David foresaw his messianic successor and wrote this psalm as a foreshadowing of the Messiah's resurrection (verses 30–31).

In spite of the fact that all of salvation history can be understood as a foreshadowing of Christ, the truth of the resurrection does not rest on a rereading of Scripture, but on the witness of Peter and the other apostles (verse 32). "All of us are witnesses," Peter said. He did the preaching, but he knew he was speaking on behalf of a community of witnesses. The corporate faith of the church in the risen Lord Jesus is a powerful witness in the world. It is this witness to the resurrection of Christ that we find throughout the Acts of the Apostles. It is the heart of the gospel and the message the world needs to hear.

Reflection and discussion

• Why was the resurrection the core of Christian preaching in Acts? Is it still the center today?

• Why are people drawn to the message of credible witnesses to the gospel of Christ? What does it take to be a believable witness to the resurrection?

Prayer

Faithful God, you do not abandon me to death but promise to raise me up to live forever with Christ. Therefore my heart is glad, my tongue rejoices, and I live always in hope.

We bring you the good news that what God promised to our ancestors he has fulfilled for us, their children, by raising Jesus. Acts 13:32–33

Paul Proclaims the Resurrection in Antioch

ACTS 13:26–43 *²⁶"My brothers, you descendants of Abraham's family, and others who fear God, to us the message of this salvation has been sent. ²⁷Because the residents of Jerusalem and their leaders did not recognize him or understand the words of the prophets that are read every sabbath, they fulfilled those words by condemning him. ²⁸Even though they found no cause for a sentence of death, they asked Pilate to have him killed. ²⁹When they had carried out everything that was written about him, they took him down from the tree and laid him in a tomb. ³⁰But God raised him from the dead; ³¹and for many days he appeared to those who came up with him from Galilee to Jerusalem, and they are now his witnesses to the people. ³²And we bring you the good news that what God promised to our ancestors ³³he has fulfilled for us, their children, by raising Jesus; as also it is written in the second psalm,*

'You are my Son;

today I have begotten you.'

³⁴As to his raising him from the dead, no more to return to corruption, he has spoken in this way,

'I will give you the holy promises made to David.'

³⁵*Therefore he has also said in another psalm,*

'You will not let your Holy One experience corruption.'
³⁶*For David, after he had served the purpose of God in his own generation, died, was laid beside his ancestors, and experienced corruption;* ³⁷*but he whom God raised up experienced no corruption.* ³⁸*Let it be known to you therefore, my brothers, that through this man forgiveness of sins is proclaimed to you;* ³⁹*by this Jesus everyone who believes is set free from all those sins from which you could not be freed by the law of Moses.* ⁴⁰*Beware, therefore, that what the prophets said does not happen to you:*

⁴¹*'Look, you scoffers!*

Be amazed and perish,

for in your days I am doing a work,

a work that you will never believe,

even if someone tells you.'"

⁴²*As Paul and Barnabas were going out, the people urged them to speak about these things again the next sabbath.* ⁴³*When the meeting of the synagogue broke up, many Jews and devout converts to Judaism followed Paul and Barnabas, who spoke to them and urged them to continue in the grace of God.*

In the second half of Acts, Paul takes center stage as a witness to Christ's resurrection. His conversion was an encounter with risen Lord, as a result of which he was commissioned to be "his witness to all the world" (Acts 22:15). In this first sermon of Paul in Acts, he speaks to those assembled in the Jewish synagogue at Antioch.

Paul first identifies himself as a member of Abraham's family, the recipients of God's "message of salvation" (verse 26). He states that their leaders in Jerusalem did not recognize Jesus as the fulfillment of God's saving plan and had him condemned to death by crucifixion (verses 27–29). But God reversed the folly of men and raised Jesus from the dead. He appeared to his followers over the course of many days, and now they are witnesses to him (verse 30–31). Paul presents himself as an evangelist, as one who brings "the good news that what God promised to our ancestors he has fulfilled for us." The focal point of that good news is the resurrection of Jesus. God has fulfilled what he had promised "by raising Jesus" (verses 32–33).

Like Peter in his Pentecost sermon, Paul demonstrates how ancient Scriptures are fulfilled in the resurrection of Jesus. He particularly notes those psalms which speak of promises made to David that obviously were not completely fulfilled in him. Psalm 2, for example, speaks of the divine sonship that David was given at his coronation, but that was fulfilled most fully in the resurrection of Jesus, the Son of God (verse 33). Likewise, Paul quotes from Psalm 16, "You will not let your Holy One experience corruption." Using the same arguments as Peter in his Pentecost sermon, Paul demonstrates that this text must apply to someone other than David, since David, in fact, is still buried in his tomb and his body experienced corruption (verses 34–36). But the body of Jesus did not decay and would never be subject to corruption (verse 37).

A new moment has dawned in God's saving plan for the world. In Christ's rising from the dead, God's forgiveness and restoration is offered to all who believe in him (verse 38–39). God's long-awaited promise for the final age is now available to all. The preaching, teaching, healings, and witness offered by Peter and Paul in Acts convince us that this is a time of new life, of rich possibilities, of restoration and resurrection. The resurrection of Jesus "from the dead" is the anticipation and foretaste of God's promise to all, the resurrection "of the dead."

Reflection and discussion

• What are the similarities between Paul's sermon in Antioch and Peter's sermon in Jerusalem?

• Why is the connection between King David and Jesus so important for both Peter and Paul?

• Luke's writings proclaim "the good news" (verse 32), both in his gospel and in Acts. What is this good news?

• How do Peter and Paul interpret the psalms in a way that demonstrates the truth of St. Augustine's words: "The New Testament is concealed in the old, and the Old Testament is made manifest in the New"?

• How would I feel if I were a member of the audience who heard these sermons in Jerusalem or Antioch? How does the good news of resurrection stir my heart today?

Prayer

God of Abraham, throughout history you have prepared your people to hear the message of salvation. Help me to hear the good news proclaimed by your apostles, and open my mind and heart to be amazed at the forgiveness and renewal you offer us through your Risen Son.

SUGGESTIONS FOR FACILITATORS, GROUP SESSION 5

1. Welcome group members and ask if anyone has any questions, announcements, or requests.

2. You may want to pray this prayer as a group:

God of the living, you raised your Son Jesus from the dead and made us his witnesses in the world. Through the inspired writings of Luke, you offer us an experience of Christ's risen presence and of the heroic deeds of the apostles. Teach us your word through the ancient prophecies and psalms of Israel, so that we can understand their completion in the Risen Messiah. Open our eyes, mind, and heart to recognize our Risen Lord, and form us into a worshiping and witnessing community of disciples.

3. Ask one or more of the following questions:
   - What insight from Luke's writings most inspired you from this week's study?
   - What new understanding of the resurrection did you learn this week?

4. Discuss lessons 19 through 24. Choose one or more of the questions for reflection and discussion from each lesson to talk over as a group.

5. Ask the group members to name one thing they have most appreciated about the way the group has worked during this Bible study. Ask group members to discuss any changes they might suggest in the way the group works in future studies.

6. Invite group members to complete lessons 25 through 30 on their own during the six days before the next meeting. They should write out their own answers to the questions as preparation for next week's session.

7. Ask the group how this study is affecting the way they look upon the resurrection and the celebration of the Lord's Day, the first day of the week.

8. Conclude by praying aloud together the prayer at the end of one of the lessons discussed. You may want to end the prayer by asking members to voice prayers of thanksgiving.

"Destroy this temple, and in three days I will raise it up." John 2:19

The New Temple of Christ's Risen Body

JOHN 2:13–22 *¹³The Passover of the Jews was near, and Jesus went up to Jerusalem. ¹⁴In the temple he found people selling cattle, sheep, and doves, and the money changers seated at their tables. ¹⁵Making a whip of cords, he drove all of them out of the temple, both the sheep and the cattle. He also poured out the coins of the money changers and overturned their tables. ¹⁶He told those who were selling the doves, "Take these things out of here! Stop making my Father's house a marketplace!" ¹⁷His disciples remembered that it was written, "Zeal for your house will consume me." ¹⁸The Jews then said to him, "What sign can you show us for doing this?" ¹⁹Jesus answered them, "Destroy this temple, and in three days I will raise it up." ²⁰The Jews then said, "This temple has been under construction for forty-six years, and will you raise it up in three days?" ²¹But he was speaking of the temple of his body. ²²After he was raised from the dead, his disciples remembered that he had said this; and they believed the scripture and the word that Jesus had spoken.*

The gospels are accounts of the life of Jesus that were written in light of his resurrection. Nothing concerning Jesus could be fully comprehended until Jesus was raised from the dead. This is particularly evident in John's gospel as the events from Jesus' life are shown to be signs pointing to a fuller understanding of who Jesus really is. The whole gospel is a progressive revelation of the glory of God's only Son who communicates the life of God to those who believe in him. Everything in the gospel leads toward Christ's resurrection and signs of the resurrection punctuate the text throughout.

As in the other three gospels, the cleansing of the temple is presented as a prophetic action. In John's gospel it is a demonstration that Jesus' ministry has to do with divine presence in the world, access to God for all, and true worship. The ancient prophets, too, had protested against the profanation of the temple and associated its purification with the messianic age (Zech 14:21; Jer 7:11). Jesus commanded the merchants to stop making the "house of my Father" into a "house of merchandise" (verse 16). For Jesus, the temple was not only a place where people gather to worship, but a place where the God of Israel, whom Jesus calls "my Father," has his dwelling. When the religious leaders asked Jesus for a verifying sign of his messianic authority (verse 18), he responded, "Destroy this temple, and in three days I will raise it up" (verse 19). Since the meaning of Jesus' words could not have been intelligible in the historical circumstances, the leaders presume that Jesus' words were a threat to destroy the magnificent temple, the construction of which had continued for the past forty-six years (verse 20).

"Remembering" in John's gospel is the process by which the community of disciples came to understand the Scriptures and the life of Jesus most fully after the resurrection. In the light of Christ's rising, the disciples read the Old Testament in a more complete way that pointed to Christ and they looked back at his words and deeds in a way that enabled them to understand their full significance. Thus, John notes that after the resurrection the disciples "remembered" the verse from Psalm 69:9, "Zeal for your house will consume me" (verse 17), and understood that it was most fulfilled in the life of Jesus. Zeal for God's dwelling place and true worship consumed his life to such a degree that it lead to his crucifixion at the hands of the temple authorities. Likewise, after the resurrection, the disciples "remembered" his words about destroying and raising the temple and understood their full meaning (verse 22). They were able to realize that Jesus was "speaking of the temple of his body" (verse 21), and that the risen body of Jesus was the new "place" in which God would be worshipped "in spirit and in truth" (John 4:23–24).

For the readers of John's gospel, the temple in Jerusalem had already been destroyed. Through the destruction and the raising of the body of Jesus, God dwells in Christ most perfectly. The new presence of God in the midst of his people was to be found in the abiding presence of the risen Christ in their midst.

Reflection and discussion

• In what way does Jesus himself completely fulfill the purpose of the temple in Jerusalem?

• What did the disciples "remember" after the resurrection of Jesus (verses 17, 22)? How does remembering help me understand Christ better?

Prayer

Father, you manifested your presence in the temple of Jerusalem to your people Israel. Help me to experience your divine presence as I worship Jesus as Lord in spirit and in truth. Let me know that I can come into your presence with trust and confidence.

Those who eat my flesh and drink my blood have eternal life, and I will raise them up on the last day; for my flesh is true food and my blood is true drink.

John 6:54–55

The Bread of Life for the Life of the World

JOHN 6:41–59 [41] *Then the Jews began to complain about him because he said, "I am the bread that came down from heaven."* [42] *They were saying, "Is not this Jesus, the son of Joseph, whose father and mother we know? How can he now say, 'I have come down from heaven'?"* [43] *Jesus answered them, "Do not complain among yourselves.* [44] *No one can come to me unless drawn by the Father who sent me; and I will raise that person up on the last day.* [45] *It is written in the prophets, 'And they shall all be taught by God.' Everyone who has heard and learned from the Father comes to me.* [46] *Not that anyone has seen the Father except the one who is from God; he has seen the Father.* [47] *Very truly, I tell you, whoever believes has eternal life.* [48] *I am the bread of life.* [49] *Your ancestors ate the manna in the wilderness, and they died.* [50] *This is the bread that comes down from heaven, so that one may eat of it and not die.* [51] *I am the living bread that came down from heaven. Whoever eats of this bread will live forever; and the bread that I will give for the life of the world is my flesh."*

[52] *The Jews then disputed among themselves, saying, "How can this man give us his flesh to eat?"* [53] *So Jesus said to them, "Very truly, I tell you, unless you eat the*

flesh of the Son of Man and drink his blood, you have no life in you. ⁵⁴*Those who eat my flesh and drink my blood have eternal life, and I will raise them up on the last day;* ⁵⁵*for my flesh is true food and my blood is true drink.* ⁵⁶*Those who eat my flesh and drink my blood abide in me, and I in them.* ⁵⁷*Just as the living Father sent me, and I live because of the Father, so whoever eats me will live because of me.* ⁵⁸*This is the bread that came down from heaven, not like that which your ancestors ate, and they died. But the one who eats this bread will live forever."* ⁵⁹*He said these things while he was teaching in the synagogue at Capernaum.*

Bread sustains human life. When the Israelites were hungry in the desert, God gave them a wondrous food for their nourishment. When they asked "What is it?" Moses said, "It is the bread that the Lord has given you to eat" (Exod 16:15). In this discourse of John's gospel, Jesus says, "I am the bread that came does from heaven." While the manna eaten by the Israelites in the wilderness sustained their lives for the journey, they eventually died (verse 49). "The living bread," which is the flesh of Jesus, provides unending life for the world (verse 51). The true bread is not manna from the sky, but the flesh-and-blood person of Christ.

Four times in rapid succession Jesus speaks of the necessity of eating his flesh and drinking his blood (verses 53–56). As is characteristic of the words of Jesus in John's gospel, the sayings have multiple levels of meaning. The flesh and blood of Jesus is his very self. To eat and drink of his very self is to participate fully in his mission and destiny, in his life and his death. Eating his body and drinking his blood is to truly be his disciple—following him, believing in him, and giving oneself with him for the life of the world. This is the nourishment that gives eternal life and victory over death.

In addition to referring to his flesh-and-blood self, the sayings of Jesus also refer to the Eucharist. Through the "true food" and "true drink" of the Eucharist (verse 55), Jesus has sustained and nourished disciples through the ages with the gift of himself. The flesh and blood of Jesus is his real, abiding presence: "Those who eat my flesh and drink my blood abide in me, and I in them" (verse 56). Eating and drinking his eucharistic presence is a sharing in his incarnate life, his sacrificial death, and his glorious life.

Jesus insists, first negatively (verse 53) and then positively (verse 54), that whoever eats his flesh and drinks his blood has eternal life now and will be raised up on the last day. The source of this life is "the living Father" who sent his Son. Christ lives because of the Father and passes on that life to those who consume him: "Whoever eats me will live because of me" (verse 57). Through belief in Jesus and sharing in the Eucharist the believer comes to eternal life and is promised resurrection. This eternal life is something we begin living now (verse 47), but also something that will achieve its fullness when we are raised on the last day (verse 44).

Reflection and discussion

• What are my deepest hungers and thirsts? How much do I trust that they will be provided for?

• What do the promises of John 6 offer to me? What do they invite me to do?

• What does Jesus ask of me as I eat his body and drink his blood?

Prayer

Lord of Life, you invite me to share deeply in your life by eating your flesh as true food and drinking your blood as true drink. Thank you for the gift of the Eucharist and for your gift of eternal life.

Martha said to him, "I know that he will rise again in the resurrection
on the last day." Jesus said to her, "I am the resurrection and the life."
John 11:24–25

Jesus Raises Lazarus to Life

JOHN 11:21–44 ²¹*Martha said to Jesus, "Lord, if you had been here, my brother would not have died. ²²But even now I know that God will give you whatever you ask of him." ²³Jesus said to her, "Your brother will rise again." ²⁴Martha said to him, "I know that he will rise again in the resurrection on the last day." ²⁵Jesus said to her, "I am the resurrection and the life. Those who believe in me, even though they die, will live, ²⁶and everyone who lives and believes in me will never die. Do you believe this?" ²⁷She said to him, "Yes, Lord, I believe that you are the Messiah, the Son of God, the one coming into the world."*

²⁸When she had said this, she went back and called her sister Mary, and told her privately, "The Teacher is here and is calling for you." ²⁹And when she heard it, she got up quickly and went to him. ³⁰Now Jesus had not yet come to the village, but was still at the place where Martha had met him. ³¹The Jews who were with her in the house, consoling her, saw Mary get up quickly and go out. They followed her because they thought that she was going to the tomb to weep there. ³²When Mary came where Jesus was and saw him, she knelt at his feet and said to him, "Lord, if you had been here, my brother would not have died." ³³When Jesus saw her weeping, and the Jews who came with her also weeping, he was greatly disturbed in spirit and deeply moved. ³⁴He said, "Where have you laid him?" They said to him, "Lord, come and see." ³⁵*Jesus began to weep.* ³⁶*So the Jews said, "See how he loved him!"* ³⁷*But some of them said, "Could not he who opened the eyes of the blind man have kept this man from dying?"*

³⁸*Then Jesus, again greatly disturbed, came to the tomb. It was a cave, and a stone was lying against it.* ³⁹*Jesus said, "Take away the stone." Martha, the sister of the dead man, said to him, "Lord, already there is a stench because he has been dead four days."* ⁴⁰*Jesus said to her, "Did I not tell you that if you believed, you would see the glory of God?"* ⁴¹*So they took away the stone. And Jesus looked upward and said, "Father, I thank you for having heard me.* ⁴²*I knew that you always hear me, but I have said this for the sake of the crowd standing here, so that they may believe that you sent me."* ⁴³*When he had said this, he cried with a loud voice, "Lazarus, come out!"* ⁴⁴*The dead man came out, his hands and feet bound with strips of cloth, and his face wrapped in a cloth. Jesus said to them, "Unbind him, and let him go."*

When Jesus tells Martha, "Your brother will rise again" (verse 23), Martha thought he was talking about "the resurrection on the last day" (verse 24). His words seemed to Martha only a pious consolation expressing the common Jewish belief in the resurrection of the just at the end of time. Like the common Christian sentiment at funerals, "He's in a better place now," the words of Jesus seem to Martha a polite sentiment that doesn't cut the grief of the moment. But Jesus has something more in mind.

Jesus said to Martha, "I am the resurrection and the life" (verse 25), expressing his identity in terms of the resurrection and eternal life he offers to us. Jesus is, first, our resurrection: "Those who believe in me, even though they die, will live" (verse 25). For those united with Jesus through faith, death will not cut them off from the life God gives and God will raise them up on the last day. Jesus is, second, our life: "Everyone who lives and believes in me will never die" (verse 26). The eternal life that we begin to experience now through faith in Jesus will never be extinguished, not even by death. Union with Jesus brings us eternal life in the present; resurrection on the last day will bring that life to its fullness. Resurrection and eternal life are the fruit of a relationship with Jesus; where Jesus is, there is life that never ends and the hope of resurrection.

The initial words of Martha and Mary are the same. They both express confidence that Jesus would have saved their brother from death had he only come to Bethany sooner (verses 21, 32). Yet, the response of Jesus to each is quite different. Responding to Martha, Jesus offers a statement of faith, an expression of his own identity as the source of resurrection and life. In response to Mary, who fell at his feet, Jesus expresses deep emotional involvement (verses 33, 35). The emotional response of Jesus suggests a mixture of deep grief and profound anger at the great enemy, death, and what death has done to his friends, Lazarus, Martha, and Mary. The believing response that Jesus offered Martha and the emotional response he offered Mary represent two necessary and complementary aspects of faith: the response of the mind and the response of the heart.

The way Lazarus emerged from the tomb, "his hands and feet bound with strips of cloth, and his face wrapped in a cloth" (verse 44), reminds us that the raising of Lazarus is far different from the resurrection of Jesus. The one who is the resurrection and the life will leave the funeral wrappings in the tomb and emerge in total freedom (20:6–7). The command of Jesus, "Unbind him, and let him go," echoes the command spoken by Moses in the name of God: "Let my people go" (Exod 5:1). God wants his people to be free from all bondage, even the final prison of death, so that we can experience the fullness of God's eternal life. Like the exodus from Egypt, the raising of Lazarus was a preview of resurrection in Christ.

Reflection and discussion

• What emotions do I experience when contemplating the reality of death?

• How would I answer the question that Jesus poses to Martha in verse 26?

• In what way are the response of the mind and the response of the heart two necessary aspects of my faith?

• What do I believe about the connection between my relationship with Jesus and my eternal destiny?

Prayer

Jesus, you are the resurrection and the life, the source of unending and glorious life forever. As I reflect on the reality of inevitable death, set me free from fear and anxiety. Help me to believe in you and to entrust my future to you.

Mary Magdalene went and announced to the disciples,
"I have seen the Lord." John 20:18

Recognizing the Risen Lord

JOHN 20:1–18 *¹Early on the first day of the week, while it was still dark, Mary Magdalene came to the tomb and saw that the stone had been removed from the tomb. ²So she ran and went to Simon Peter and the other disciple, the one whom Jesus loved, and said to them, "They have taken the Lord out of the tomb, and we do not know where they have laid him." ³Then Peter and the other disciple set out and went toward the tomb. ⁴The two were running together, but the other disciple outran Peter and reached the tomb first. ⁵He bent down to look in and saw the linen wrappings lying there, but he did not go in. ⁶Then Simon Peter came, following him, and went into the tomb. He saw the linen wrappings lying there, ⁷and the cloth that had been on Jesus' head, not lying with the linen wrappings but rolled up in a place by itself. ⁸Then the other disciple, who reached the tomb first, also went in, and he saw and believed; ⁹for as yet they did not understand the scripture, that he must rise from the dead. ¹⁰Then the disciples returned to their homes.*

¹¹But Mary stood weeping outside the tomb. As she wept, she bent over to look into the tomb; ¹²and she saw two angels in white, sitting where the body of Jesus had been lying, one at the head and the other at the feet. ¹³They said to her, "Woman, why are you weeping?" She said to them, "They have taken away my Lord, and I do not know where they have laid him." ¹⁴When she had said this, she turned around and saw Jesus standing there, but she did not know that it was Jesus. ¹⁵*Jesus said to her, "Woman, why are you weeping? Whom are you looking for?" Supposing him to be the gardener, she said to him, "Sir, if you have carried him away, tell me where you have laid him, and I will take him away."* ¹⁶*Jesus said to her, "Mary!" She turned and said to him in Hebrew, "Rabbouni!" (which means Teacher).* ¹⁷*Jesus said to her, "Do not hold on to me, because I have not yet ascended to the Father. But go to my brothers and say to them, 'I am ascending to my Father and your Father, to my God and your God.'"* ¹⁸*Mary Magdalene went and announced to the disciples, "I have seen the Lord"; and she told them that he had said these things to her.*

The resurrection narratives of John's gospel begin in the predawn darkness (verse 1), symbolizing the darkness of the world apart from Jesus. The disciples had not yet experienced the light of faith in the resurrection. But the darkness cannot overcome the light of the world (John 1:5). On this "first day of the week" the new creation had begun. In the "word made flesh" (John 1:14), Creator and creation came together as one. Now in the resurrection, Creator and new creation become one.

When Mary Magdalene saw the stone rolled to one side and presumably looked in to discover that the tomb was empty, her immediate reaction was to assume that the body of Jesus had been removed by some unknown persons (verse 2). Mary had come to the tomb fully expecting to see the corpse of Jesus, and it is important to note that the empty tomb did not lead her to the conclusion that Jesus had risen from the dead.

Peter and "the other disciple" then race to the tomb (verse 3). The disciple "whom Jesus loved" has the edge both in speed and insight. Though arriving at the tomb first, the beloved disciple does not go in, but defers to Peter. By noting Peter's entry into the tomb first, the gospel writer shows he is familiar with the dominant resurrection tradition that Peter is the chief witness of the resurrection. In the tomb Peter saw the linen wrapping and the cloth that had covered the head of Jesus (verses 6–7). It must have seemed very strange to see the grave clothes without the body. If Mary had been correct in assuming the corpse had been removed, this would mean that the grave-robbers had undressed the corpse, a useless and desecrating gesture. But the response of the beloved disciple was quite different from the other two. When he went inside the tomb, "he saw and believed" (verse 8). Always presented in the gospel as a model of belief, the beloved disciple examines the evidence and draws the correct conclusion.

Mary Magdalene's difficulty in recognizing the risen Jesus demonstrates that the reality of Jesus had changed; his followers now experience him in a new way. The scene is charged with intimacy and affection. Mary is overwhelmed by her loss; her tears are those of a woman who truly loved Jesus (verse 11). When Jesus asks, "Woman, why are you weeping? For whom are you looking?" Mary fails to recognize him (verses 14–15). Only when Jesus calls her by name does she recognize him (verse 16). Until now, Mary has "seen" Jesus, but not really looked at him with her full attention. But the calling of her name creates that personal bond that establishes belief. Instinctively, Mary then embraces Jesus. But Jesus gently asks her not to "hold on" to him because he had not yet returned to the Father (verse 17). She is trying to hold on to Jesus in the same way she would cling to an ordinary human. Jesus indicates that his permanent presence will come only with the gift of the Spirit as he ascends to the Father.

When Mary proclaims, "I have seen the Lord" (verse 18), she is referring to an experience far deeper and more real than simply a visual sighting. The experience is one of loving recognition, a deeply personal and mystical encounter. Mary Magdalene has moved from the darkness to the light of faith. She has seen Jesus as Lord, and she cannot help but become the messenger of that good news to others.

Reflection and discussion

• What is the difference in the way the disciples experienced the "resuscitated" Lazarus and the risen Jesus?

• What is the difference between the responses of Peter and the beloved disciple? Which of them is more like me?

• What strikes me most about the encounter between Jesus and Mary Magdalene? How is it much more than a visual sighting?

• How is Mary Magdalene a model of faith for me?

Prayer

Risen Lord, you are the beginning of God's new creation, the light that shines in the world's darkness. Give me the energy to run to you and the insight to experience your risen presence. Call me by name to experience a deep communion of life with you.

"Unless I see the mark of the nails in his hands, and put my finger in the mark of the nails and my hand in his side, I will not believe." John 20:25

Moving from Doubt to Belief

JOHN 20:19–31 ¹⁹*When it was evening on that day, the first day of the week, and the doors of the house where the disciples had met were locked for fear of the Jews, Jesus came and stood among them and said, "Peace be with you." ²⁰After he said this, he showed them his hands and his side. Then the disciples rejoiced when they saw the Lord. ²¹Jesus said to them again, "Peace be with you. As the Father has sent me, so I send you." ²²When he had said this, he breathed on them and said to them, "Receive the Holy Spirit. ²³If you forgive the sins of any, they are forgiven them; if you retain the sins of any, they are retained."*

²⁴*But Thomas (who was called the Twin), one of the twelve, was not with them when Jesus came. ²⁵So the other disciples told him, "We have seen the Lord." But he said to them, "Unless I see the mark of the nails in his hands, and put my finger in the mark of the nails and my hand in his side, I will not believe."*

²⁶*A week later his disciples were again in the house, and Thomas was with them. Although the doors were shut, Jesus came and stood among them and said, "Peace be with you." ²⁷Then he said to Thomas, "Put your finger here and*

see my hands. Reach out your hand and put it in my side. Do not doubt but believe." ²⁸*Thomas answered him, "My Lord and my God!"* ²⁹*Jesus said to him, "Have you believed because you have seen me? Blessed are those who have not seen and yet have come to believe."*

³⁰*Now Jesus did many other signs in the presence of his disciples, which are not written in this book.* ³¹*But these are written so that you may come to believe that Jesus is the Messiah, the Son of God, and that through believing you may have life in his name.*

The appearance of the risen Jesus moves the disciples from a state of fear behind locked doors (verse 19) to the experience of joy and wonderment. The Lord's greeting, "Peace be with you" (verses 19, 21), was a common Hebrew salutation. Yet hearing those words on the lips of the one who suffered and died, and now stands among them, gave them a new richness. Peace (in Hebrew, *shalom*) is not just the absence of conflict; it is an experience of deep confidence that dispels fear and is full of hope. The disciples remembered his words spoken in the upper room before his death: "Peace I leave with you; my peace I give to you. Do not let your hearts be troubled, and do not let them be afraid" (14:27).

After his first greeting of peace, Jesus showed them his hands and his side. They knew that the risen one was not a phantom, but the same Jesus who was lifted up on the cross. After his second greeting of peace, Jesus sent his disciples on their mission: "As the Father has sent me, so I send you" (verse 21). Because God so loved the world, he sent his Son (3:16) who revealed the Father for all to see—through his teachings, his healing signs, and finally through his total self-gift on the cross. Now Jesus sends us, his disciples, on that same mission. We are to be for the world what Jesus has been for the world. We are to embody the Father's love, to teach and heal, to comfort and bring peace, to love as Jesus loved.

To empower the disciples to carry out their mission Jesus breathed on them and said, "Receive the Holy Spirit" (verse 22). Just as the Father had sent out Jesus in the power of the Spirit, so now Jesus sends out his disciples in the power of the Spirit. Much as the Creator breathed life into the first human beings (Gen 2:7) or Ezekiel prophesied to the "breath" to revive the dry bones of his vision (Ezek 37), Jesus breathed his Spirit into God's new creation, the community of disciples empowered to forgive, heal, teach, and love.

Thomas had missed the appearance of Christ to the other disciples, and he would not believe the others when they told him, "We have seen the Lord" (verse 25). Unlike the disciples the previous week, for whom seeing was believing, for Thomas, more was required: he wanted tangible proof of the resurrection. When Jesus appeared again and invited Thomas to touch his wounded hands and his side, Thomas's doubts disappeared. His skepticism is transformed into the supreme profession of Christian faith: "My Lord and my God" (verse 28). Jesus is given many titles throughout the gospel of John: Word of God, Rabbi, Messiah, Prophet, King of Israel, Son of God, and others. Yet nothing more profound could be said of him than Thomas's climactic exclamation and affirmation of Christ's divinity. For many like Thomas, doubt is the pathway to belief. For those who struggle with their faith, Thomas is a model. The most confounded cynic can become the most jubilant believer of all.

Reflection and discussion

• What indications are given in this appearance narrative that the risen body of Jesus is real?

• Describe the work of the Father, Son, and Holy Spirit in the mission of the church (verses 21–22).

- In what specific way can I continue the mission of Jesus this day?

- In what ways does Thomas give me hope for my struggles with faith?

- What is the author's purpose in writing this gospel? How is this gospel more than a biography of Jesus?

Prayer

Wounded and risen Jesus, let me know the peace and joy of your resurrection in every part of my life. Empower me with your Holy Spirit and send me to offer your compassion, forgiveness, and healing to others.

**Simon Peter went aboard and hauled the net ashore,
full of large fish, a hundred fifty-three of them;
and though there were so many, the net was not torn.** John 21:11

Catching Fish at the Lord's Command

JOHN 21:1–14 ¹*After these things Jesus showed himself again to the disciples by the Sea of Tiberias; and he showed himself in this way.* ²*Gathered there together were Simon Peter, Thomas called the Twin, Nathanael of Cana in Galilee, the sons of Zebedee, and two others of his disciples.* ³*Simon Peter said to them, "I am going fishing." They said to him, "We will go with you." They went out and got into the boat, but that night they caught nothing.*

⁴*Just after daybreak, Jesus stood on the beach; but the disciples did not know that it was Jesus.* ⁵*Jesus said to them, "Children, you have no fish, have you?" They answered him, "No."* ⁶*He said to them, "Cast the net to the right side of the boat, and you will find some." So they cast it, and now they were not able to haul it in because there were so many fish.* ⁷*That disciple whom Jesus loved said to Peter, "It is the Lord!" When Simon Peter heard that it was the Lord, he put on some clothes, for he was naked, and jumped into the sea.* ⁸*But the other disciples came in the boat, dragging the net full of fish, for they were not far from the land, only about a hundred yards off.*

⁹*When they had gone ashore, they saw a charcoal fire there, with fish on it, and bread.* ¹⁰*Jesus said to them, "Bring some of the fish that you have just*

117

caught." [11]*So Simon Peter went aboard and hauled the net ashore, full of large fish, a hundred fifty-three of them; and though there were so many, the net was not torn.* [12]*Jesus said to them, "Come and have breakfast." Now none of the disciples dared to ask him, "Who are you?" because they knew it was the Lord.* [13]*Jesus came and took the bread and gave it to them, and did the same with the fish.* [14]*This was now the third time that Jesus appeared to the disciples after he was raised from the dead.*

Nowhere in the resurrection accounts of the gospels do people go looking for the risen Jesus. His appearance is always unanticipated. In this account, the disciples had returned to Galilee. They had not gone to look for Jesus; they were looking for fish. Like thousands of other pilgrims, they had returned home after the Passover festival in Jerusalem. Back in their own haunts, they returned to what they knew best—fishing. The fact that Jesus "showed himself" (verse 1) to them, when and where they least expected it, emphasizes the reality of the resurrection.

The futility of the disciples' fishing efforts during the night, followed by their tremendous success in the morning light with Jesus present, continues the contrast between darkness and light so typical of this gospel. Without Jesus they catch nothing (verse 3). With his direction the catch is overwhelming (verse 6). It would have been tempting for Peter and his friends to ignore the advice of Jesus. They had been fishing all night and must have been exhausted. But Jesus encouraged them to give it another shot and to do it differently this time. The result was an overflowing net: "They were not able to haul it in because there were so many fish." The great catch occurred not just because the fish were there, but because the risen Lord was there with his authority and power. The record-breaking catch is the catalyst to recognition. The beloved disciple said to Peter, "It is the Lord" (verse 7).

The record-breaking catch symbolically represents the apostolic mission Jesus gives to his disciples. After the great catch in Luke's gospel, Jesus tells his disciples, "From now on you will be catching people" (Luke 5:10). Based on the commentary of St. Jerome that holds there were 153 known varieties of fish at the time, the overwhelming number of "large fish" represents the universality and all-embracing character of the mission (verse 11). The great catch is the symbolic equivalent of the great commission Jesus gives his followers at the end of Matthew's gospel: "Go and make disciples of all nations"(Matt 28:19).

Reflection and discussion

• In what ways has Jesus made my work successful and fruitful by urging me to try again and do it differently?

• In what way does fishing represent the mission Jesus gave to his disciples?

• In what ways have I unexpectedly experienced the presence of the risen Christ? How is it possible to believe without seeing?

Prayer

Glorious Christ, give me the intuition and insight to recognize your presence today. Bring your light into my darkness, give me confidence in my work, and give me the love to accomplish the mission you give me this day.

SUGGESTIONS FOR FACILITATORS, GROUP SESSION 6

1. Welcome group members and make any final announcements or requests.

2. You may want to pray this prayer as a group:

Lord Jesus, you revealed yourself as the resurrection and the life, our source of eternal life now and our hope of future resurrection. Through the inspired words of the Gospel of John, you reveal your glory and communicate divine life to those who believe in you. Your glorified presence is the new temple where God dwells among us and where we can worship God in spirit and in truth. Move us from darkness to the light of faith, and encourage us to be messengers of the good news of resurrection.

3. Ask one or more of the following questions:
   - In what way has this study challenged you the most?
   - What words do you think of now when you think about resurrection?

4. Discuss lessons 25 through 30. Choose one or more of the questions for reflection and discussion from each lesson to discuss as a group.

5. Ask the group if they would like to study another book in the Threshold Bible Study series. Discuss the topic and dates, and make a decision among those interested. Ask the group members to suggest people they would like to invite to participate in the next study series.

6. Ask the group to discuss the insights that stand out most from this study over the past six weeks and how the resurrection will hold a richer meaning from now on.

7. Conclude by praying aloud the following prayer or another of your own choosing:

Holy Spirit of God, you inspired the sacred writers of the Bible and you have guided our study during these weeks. Continue to deepen our love for the word of God in the holy Scriptures and draw us to the risen life you have promised. Enliven us with the resurrected life of Christ so that we can be witnesses to his resurrection to the world. Bless us with the fire of your love.

Ordering Additional Studies

AVAILABLE TITLES IN THIS SERIES INCLUDE...

Advent Light • Angels of God • Eucharist
The Feasts of Judaism • The Holy Spirit and Spiritual Gifts
Jerusalem, the Holy City • The Lamb and the Beasts
Mysteries of the Rosary • The Names of Jesus
People of the Passion • Pilgrimage in the Footsteps of Jesus
The Resurrection and the Life • The Sacred Heart of Jesus
Stewardship of the Earth • The Tragic and Triumphant Cross

Jesus, the Messianic King (Part 1): Matthew 1–16
Jesus, the Messianic King (Part 2): Matthew 17–28
Jesus, the Suffering Servant (Part 1): Mark 1–8
Jesus, the Suffering Servant (Part 2): Mark 9–16
Jesus, the Word Made Flesh (Part 1): John 1–10
Jesus, the Word Made Flesh (Part 2): John 11–21

UPCOMING TITLES

Church of the Holy Spirit (Part 1): Acts of the Apostles 1–14
Church of the Holy Spirit (Part 2): Acts of the Apostles 15–28
Jesus, the Compassionate Savior (Part 1): Luke 1–11
Jesus, the Compassionate Savior (Part 2): Luke 12–24

To check availability or for a description
of each study, visit our website at
www.ThresholdBibleStudy.com
or call us at **1-800-321-0411**

TWENTY
THIRD 23rd
PUBLICATIONS